DO I HAVE TO BE GOOD ALL THE TIME?

RIVER
PUBLISHING

VICKY WALKER

River Publishing & Media Ltd
Barham Court
Teston
Maidstone
Kent
ME18 5BZ
United Kingdom

info@river-publishing.co.uk

ISBN 978-1-908393-13-5

Printed in the United Kingdom

Contents

Dedication

To my family, who are pretty great actually

Acknowledgements

I would like to say a heartfelt thanks to all those lovely friends and kindly people who shared their thoughts, questions, wonderings and lives with me and inspired this book. All names from here onwards have been changed to protect the innocent – and not so – but you know who you are. Grateful thanks too to those who read my scribbles in the early stages and gave great feedback which helped to form this into something almost comprehensible, and those understanding and supportive folk who bought me dinners and got excited on my behalf. Thank you Tim Pettingale at River Publishing for making it happen!

Introduction

Why me?

I will confess it all now. I've checked the covers of a lot of God books, studied those smiling faces and neat biographies and I don't match up. I did not marry my childhood sweetheart (maybe because I didn't have one). Nor the boy next door (contrary to notions gathered from romantic movies, he was only six and had braces). Nor a nice young man from the university Christian Union (CU? More like c u later). Nor a hard-working, sincere pastory type (they are mostly spoken for by the age of twenty anyway. I think there's some sort of law). Nor anyone, to date.

I don't have a brood of adorable children with appropriately biblical names. I don't come from generations of God-fearing, wholesome folk who never veered from the straight and narrow.

I can count among my family members, past and present, a pantomime dame (retired), a Gary Glitter impersonator (how times have changed), a showgirl (now showing very little these days), a naked dancer (thankfully showing a little less than before. Most of the time), a music hall comedian and acrobat, and a librarian (well, you can't have it all). I have never started a prayer chain or held a women's Bible study in my home or built a school in a developing country, or any of the things that seem to be required for level 1 modern-day faith. Well, level 2 maybe. I think level 1 just involves not being frightened off enough to stick around.

So what have I done? I've lived life, as best I could – and met lots of other people along the way, trying to figure it out too. Made mistakes, and wondered if I'm the only one who has done such things, and whether there is an encyclopaedia of original sin so I can see if I've actually made it. Enjoyed myself and wondered if that was appropriate as no one was singing hymns at the time. I've left it all behind for a few years and wandered the world, wondering if there was more satisfaction to be found doing what I wanted rather than what I thought I should. And I've come back. And met people who have wondered the same things, and if they are in the right place, and if they told people what was really going on in their lives, or even just in their minds, whether anyone would speak to them again. And I thought, if any of the things I've done, talked about, heard about or even wondered about would help anyone, I'd write them down. So I did.

Does that mean you should immediately cast aside this book and spend several days and nights praying for your soul? Probably not. As far as I can ascertain, my silliness isn't infectious. And I don't claim to speak on behalf of anyone else, so probably no point in alerting your local bishop. I'm human (almost 100 per cent, according to recent tests) so very likely to say at least a couple of things that might cause a raised eyebrow, but no intentional offence, I promise.

And I'm not intending to classify myself with a neat label, so there is absolutely no need to panic if you are single, married or anywhere in between and fearing you might be led astray. We're all in this together, even if it doesn't always seem that way. From the outside, it can be all too easy to look around and notice the differences and not what we've got in common. Young mum, long-time married, never been kissed, ever hopeful – could we all actually be experiencing at least some of the same things? Even just wondering what might be going on in the lives of those people who seem so different to us? And what about the twists and turns of life that can happen to anyone, but perhaps don't get talked about much? Am I the only one with such things running through my fevered imagination?

So that's all this is. A little bit of thinking out loud about some of the things we might all have pondered: love and romance, temptation, that mysterious thing called grace, control and pride. From what I've heard whispered we're not immune to any of it because of our age or status. But even if it seems a million miles from our own lives, maybe sneaking a little glimpse behind someone else's confident façade could be interesting. Don't be fooled by the brave faces, perfect grooming or even the spiritual certainties – deep down I suspect we're all asking at least some of the same questions. So why not sit back, read on and feel extremely thankful, perhaps even a tiny bit smug, that you've never done any of the silly things I'm about to tell you. I, for one, will choose to believe you. Until we know each other a little bit better anyway...

1. If love is heaven sent, does that mean I can't send it back?

I think I'm a little bit selfish.

Just a little bit.

Much as I express, and genuinely feel, happiness for those who find eternal joy in each other's arms, there is a tiny part of me that would be equally happy to let them get on with it, no witnesses, no questions asked. But it doesn't seem to work that way, does it? True love likes an audience, ideally an audience bearing gifts from a specially selected department store list. Ever been at a wedding that seemed to transcend the rules of time? Incessant toasts, speeches designed to break world records, bridesmaids missing in action under mounds of confetti? Suspicions the young lovers would be celebrating their first anniversary before we'd actually left the reception? The three-day ceremony at which I was once a guest must surely qualify. I was there plus none, friend of no one but the bride and groom – who, thoughtlessly, were too busy being centre of attention to entertain me – and was trying my hardest to embrace the spirit of the occasion. But for some, like castaways on Random Wedding Island, driven mad by the small talk and the harsh beating down of the disco lights, it was all too much. Nuptial-induced trauma led to highly inappropriate utterings, and – for once – it wasn't me.

I had been seated next to another friend of the happy couple. A charming and friendly chap who spent the weekend regaling me with tales of his life, work, relationships, the whole package. He was single, animated (not in the Mickey Mouse sense) and actively pursuing further conversation at every opportunity. It was towards the end of the second day, after we had danced, laughed and he had impulsively let me drive his very, very (very) expensive car around town when proceedings had dragged during yet another wait between rituals, that he got to talking about what he liked to do when he got in from work of an evening. It was general and unsurprising stuff, mentioned only to fill in yet more waiting around time: TV, dinner, that kind of thing. And then, apparently caught up in the moment, he carried on a little further...

"And then I like to lie down, take off my shirt and have my cats crawl all over my bare chest."

There was a long, long (long) pause. Then he spoke very slowly, without raising his eyes from the table.

"I've just said too much, haven't I?"

I could only stare at the table too, and nod, as the mental images refused to dissipate. We never spoke again. Not even to pass on special offers on Whiskas.

OK, so it didn't happen for me and Mr Kit-e-kat, but let's just think about it for a moment. The wonderful, joyous experience of true love. Is there anything like it? Whom God has joined together, till death do us part. Sex, romance, beautiful moments and all of that... what could possibly go wrong? I mean, isn't the idea of it just so perfect? Commitment, companionship, passion, the coming together of two lives to create one new one. Like Adam and Eve in our own personal paradise. Is that what we all want? What if maybe you don't? But if you do, there's just one small issue. Meeting someone. Or should I say, the right someone.

Who said, "Just be yourself"?

It can be very easy to make a less than stunning first impression. I'm sure I've just blocked out the memories of most of my own faux pas (I mean, it's much more likely that I've never done anything silly when meeting someone for the first time, of course...) but so many people have told me of the ridiculous things they've said and done in order to impress, or even just break the ice, there must be something in it. Cringing that lasts for years, increasing with every retelling. I've heard it over and over again.

Like the oh-so-English man who wanted to impress a woman he saw on holiday in France. Approaching with his best GCSE-standard introduction rehearsed, he launched into a flamboyant "Ah, bonjour. Ça va?" accompanied by flourishes and a knowing smile. The woman looked at him, opened her mouth to speak, paused for a moment and then said, "Oui, ça va. Et vous?"

Emboldened, he carried on, pulling on every linguistic trick he could think of, confidence growing with each exotic syllable. She had what could be described as a smirk on her face. He just assumed she was very pleased by his efforts – he must be better at this than he thought. Perhaps she thought he was local! It didn't take long, though, before he had run out of things to say and tried for one last sentence before admitting defeat. By this time she was grinning widely. She tried to suppress it but failed. "I could answer you in French again, but seeing as we're both English shall we just revert to that? Save your brain from hurting?"

It turned out they even lived in the same town – and had met before. At a party. Where he had been rude to her. And she had instantly recognised him, even in the glorious Gallic sunshine. C'est la vie.

At what point will I need a dowry?

I think it's harder in Christian circles (which sometimes seem to be filled with Christian squares). Not only is there the general expectation of our minds being on higher things, but there are strange new standards to live up to, which can be bewildering and hard to decipher. What is it appropriate to say if you like the look of someone? Is it even appropriate to like the look of someone? We are often encouraged to make a long list of all the qualities we want in a partner, rather like a job description though extending to every aspect of character and personality. It seems that it may now be necessary to actually interview people to find out if they measure up. Had that experience yet? Maybe it's just me. Me the interviewee, not the interviewer, that is. Come on, surely I'm not the only one?

Over the years, more so lately, I've unexpectedly found myself on the receiving end of a range of pointed questions. Questions about my child-bearing plans/ability, about my propensity or not to put on weight, about my general lifestyle, habits and churchliness. All of this is book-ended by a brief bio from the man asking the questions, outlining his general devotion to God and aims and aspirations in that direction, and somewhere a summary of his expectations of marriage and relationships. It's a small miracle lawyers aren't involved, even at the first interaction. Christians may have given up dating after meeting in person if some recent publications are anything to go by, but the Newsnight-style interview process masquerading as romantic interest can replace it in one easy step. Why meet someone and get to know them over time when you can call them up and speedily turn the conversation round to their potential as your life partner? It's all over in twenty minutes. I've become attuned to the signs. The reason for the call is a pretext. Within a couple of minutes the real agenda becomes apparent.

I've started so I'll finish

To be fair it's happened face to face too. Sometimes a drink, or even a meal, has been involved. But the process is always similar. Rather than a relaxed, getting-to-know-you chat or a genuinely interesting, deep conversation, allowing for real personalities to surface, the not remotely subtle questioning is dropped in at every turn. It's rather off-putting. It isn't unheard of for the target of the inquiry to be unaware they are being considered for a life-changing role if previous contact has been limited to the purely friendly. Nice people they may be, but what happened to chemistry, attraction, humour, fun, variety, depth? How spontaneous is someone going to be in life if they approach a potential partner with a pre-prepared questionnaire? And how tempting is it to cheat in the answers we give on this particular test?

I will confess that I have done it. That anyone who has tried the interview process on me has found the interrogation not going to plan. As they have probed for information, I have counteracted with answers calculated to be as far away from their ideal answer as I can plausibly make them. The answers are still true: they are just worded not to play the game.

If the desired response is that I come across as a laid-back and freewheeling hippy chick, my most high-maintenance qualities come to the fore. If I am expected to comply with a personal grooming routine to rival Victoria Beckham's, I emphasise my low-maintenance side. If I am asked if I'm naturally thin or have to work at it (yes, really), I ask what it has to do with them. Usually while staring at their waistline. If they don't want an actual conversation, I'm just not playing. I don't want to impress someone who has a list. I'm not after a gold star.

Old blue eyes

Granted this is not just a Christian trait. Bonnie was once told by a nice young man that she had all the qualities on his list and he thus foresaw their relationship being long lasting and productive. I think it may have been her first experience of "the list" and she just had to know what was on it. He went through it all, every personal requirement. It was a perfect match – until he got to eye colour (yes, that specific). She let him finish and then informed him she didn't have eyes of that colour. He leaned forward to see for himself. He put on a brighter light to be extra sure. Then he leaned back, weighed the situation for some time, and finally spoke. The tone was serious and considered.

"I'm prepared to let that go."

Funnily enough, she wasn't.

How much does this approach allow for people to just be themselves? Original, unique, multi-faceted. Not to mention fallible, changeable, less than perfect. The Christian world may demand higher, and very specific, standards for partners, but could it be that we're just not getting past the surface and seeing people as they really are? By wanting it all to line up neatly from the outset, are we setting ourselves up for disappointment and missing a desperately needed reality check? People, even Christians (gasp. Who just fainted?), don't come in neat packages with the loose ends all tied up. We just don't. We are all a lot deeper than that, and we owe it to ourselves not to be going down a road of superficiality or out-dated stereotypes.

Nor should we hide behind what we think people want to hear. I heard somewhere that eight weeks into a new relationship there is some sign of the partner's negative traits. This, apparently, is how long it takes before the mask slips, before we revert to type, even briefly, and start to reveal the things we want to hide. It could be perfectly innocuous stuff, or it could be more significant, or even sinister. Can we allow ourselves to be more vulnerable than that? To be ourselves, flaws and quirks on show, rather than trying to present an idealised version of ourselves? If we're doing it, and they're doing it too, what do we actually have at the end of it except a big, fat, fake waste of time?

A walk on the Why side

One, now happily married, friend used to take her potential paramours on a long walk around a particular route. Twelve miles long and no short cuts. During that time, conversation would get past the basics, past the glib and well-rehearsed answers. She would see how they behaved when they got tired, or if it rained. She would get an insight into much more than what they wanted her to see. On one occasion she carried the picnic basket with both lunches the whole way round as her gentleman companion was too tired. Funnily enough, he didn't qualify for another walking date. Getting to know people is crucial. We may really want to meet the partner of our dreams, but what chance do we have if we don't actually get to know anyone? I don't just mean people we might fancy a bit, I mean anyone. Develop a wide social circle. Instead we're ruling people out before we even start. Assuming we know the answer before we've considered the question.

Concentrating our efforts on matching up our (or our church's) interpretation of the ideal partner with the motley crew we meet in the Christian world, we can end up forcing our expectations on people who may be suitable or not, but don't get past our first self-imposed hurdle. Are we only seeing them as potential partners or nothing at all? Are they the only categories we entertain? What happened to just being people together, brothers and sisters, before anything else?

Under the Christian magnifying glass, smaller details can seem huge. Men and women who don't have much interaction with the opposite sex can read significance into anything, no matter how incidental. Within the setting of official church meetings and groups, everything can come veiled with spirituality. Out loud, anyway. Do our thoughts match up? Do we ever have normal conversations which take us to a different level, not just small talk? Do we talk "spiritual" and never get past the surface? Are we busy pigeonholing people without actually getting to know them? Do we misinterpret friendliness as something more?

Dream lover

In a recent conversation about church life, talk turned to a young female member. A low-key, naturally pretty girl who always seemed to be smiling. One of the men in the group, unsure if he was thinking of the right person, asked if she was "the pretty, flirtatious one". "Hmm," I answered, "she is pretty. But flirtatious…

what makes you say that?"

"Well," he replied, "she's just very friendly, isn't she? And dresses in pretty, feminine clothes."

I still couldn't understand how this equalled flirtatiousness. She was over twenty years younger than him and it was obvious she wasn't harbouring any secret romantic interest. And yet, in his mind, she was flirting. He believed her behaviour was designed to interest and attract him. Wishful thinking? I suspect so. Projection of his desires onto her? Maybe. What could she do to avoid the accusation? Be less friendly? Less pretty? She was one of the least overt girls I've ever met, in or out of church. Her demeanour was understated rather than outgoing. To avoid future misunderstanding she has now taken to wearing a full veil and avoiding eye contact for the sake of all involved (OK, not really).

Maybe church was one of the few places this man had friendly contact with women he found attractive, and he was unsure what to make of such exchanges. Maybe church didn't address male-female interactions or provide realistic expectations. It seems hard for men and women to know how to relate to each other and where the boundaries are. As many leaders are married, and often marry young, it can be difficult to know what to do with people who don't arrive in a neat couple. Have them tag along with the throng of happy lovers like holy gooseberries? Hope they are the kind that like a lot of solitary time, except for an increased availability to assist with church volunteering and prayer meetings at unsociable hours? Pack them all off under the banner of "Singles" and hope it somehow works itself out? I guess some churches are better equipped, having a large enough contingent of single people for social activity to be effortless, but not all are like that. I've been in churches where the solo travellers are clearly the minority and very much out on a limb. Not much fun.

And for the unattached people, can a lot of time spent in church result in forgetting how to communicate with the opposite sex in normal ways? The level of mystery that is created through unspoken sexual stereotyping and distance can lead to a monumental lack of perspective. Overwhelming significance can be given to minor exchanges, and often at the expense of real relationships. Throw in the great unmentionable of sexual frustration and this can lead to isolation, loneliness, missed opportunities and even a lack of moving on in life. We get stuck looking with our noses pressed up against the shop window, if we even bother looking at all. We miss opportunities for all kinds of other interactions, not just the one we are pinning all our hopes on.

Lesley had spent years wanting a Christian husband. Almost all her friends were female and most of them were in the same situation. As time went by and she hadn't met anyone who fulfilled her list – which gradually became longer and longer – she became frustrated. Conversations with friends were dominated by the topic. When she met men socially, she would check them off against her requirements, and they never quite matched up. If they were friendly, she would become wary. She might even withdraw and confide later that she could tell they wanted more than friendship, that she wasn't interested and didn't want to encourage them. It would later turn out that there wasn't any ulterior motive, but it was then too late for friendships to develop. Sometimes, if they were close enough to ticking all the boxes for her to be prepared to investigate further, she would wait for them to pursue her. Oblivious to her expectation, they didn't.

It can get tricky. Gloria told me that heading off on a church weekend away the only lift she could find was with a single man from her church. During the four-hour drive she mentally tortured herself that God intended her to marry him. Why? Because it was the most time she had spent one to one with a man in several years. And I'm happy to tell you she was right! And they've just celebrated their tenth anniversary! Just kidding, I don't think they ever spoke again.

First impressions, second chances

For some Christians it seems genuinely hard to put away out-dated biblical references to love, relationships and marriage. Don't read that wrongly – I'm not saying we shouldn't have God at the centre of what we aspire to find in a partner, even in our friendships. I'm just suggesting that, instead of a checklist, we consider getting to know people based on how God sees them, not how we see them. It seems to be people, not God, who set immovable benchmarks for perfect partners. In all my years in church, I've not yet met anyone perfect (I know, I've never been to your church and I've never met you. It could all be so different). No one has come close to a Jesus-like flawlessness, no matter how hard they've tried. They've hurt people, disappointed them, let them down, been selfish, not made the effort they should, shouted, snapped, sworn, avoided, resented, judged – the list is endless. I should know – I'm describing myself. How can anyone like that hope to score high on a tick list? If you want to make the requirements black and white, make the shortcomings the same – and expect relationships to die out very quickly, if they even get to start.

If you want to do away with the rigidity, and open up the prospect of depth and variety, expect to be surprised, probably pleasantly and negatively. Expect to have experiences instead of just trying to make it all match up. We can't get involved with anyone without embracing risk. We will get hurt. We will cause hurt. And we won't mean to do it. A list of compulsory qualities won't change that. To get to know people and let them get to know us is costly. It takes our time, our energy, our commitment, vulnerability, boldness not to withdraw when there are differences of opinion, grace not to take offence, sensitivity not to cause it. And in case you haven't realised by now, I'm talking about all relationships, not just the romantic. For many of us, romantic relationships may not even figure. Does that mean that our other interactions should lack depth? Or can we have something different?

Through the holy looking glass

How does anyone go about understanding relationships in the Christian world? Especially when coming into it from another place, where the rules are different, if there are any rules at all. It can seem contradictory.

While we should be close – brothers and sisters, apparently – we also should perhaps be keeping our distance. Where, for those coming into church from the everyday world, the focus seems to have shifted onto things you may have thought no one bothered about any more.

Are you really expected to chaperone grown men and women on so-called dates, because they don't want to be alone? (Or maybe they do, and that's the problem.) Where couples who've just met start telling you their wedding plans, when couples you know out in the world are living together, having babies and thinking about marriage some time never. What to make of all that?

The recent popularity of Christian books on purity and lust has highlighted opinions held by some that "worldly" ways may be creeping into churches. Here I become a little wary.

Do I sense some preaching heading our way? Extremes are being spoken of, and Christians are asked to choose which side they're on. Watch out, lust's about. And how is this manifesting?

Watch out, naughty ladies about...

Generally men are feeling tempted by women. Yes, there are some concessions that women may be feeling tempted too, but often it's men writing about men and women and sex who have noticed that men are the ones being put under duress.

And the underlying tone is that girls cannot relax, lest they become one of "those" girls...

That friendly hug you give? Well, the recipient may be loving it in a less than brotherly way, sister.

The fact you laugh and chat with men after church? Hmm, what's really going on in your mind – or theirs?

That top you like? Have you realised what it's doing to the men who can see a little midriff?

Your hair, your clothes, your appearance, your general existence – what effect are they having?

And more importantly, what kind of girl are you? Are you someone that a good Christian man would want to marry? (Eek, do I sense a list creeping up on us again?)

I've been around church life for years and it makes me uneasy. For women coming into the church for the first time having lived life outside it, never mind those who have lived for years knowing both worlds, this can create unnecessary pressure. I'm not suggesting for a moment that Christian women (or men) should be indulging in manipulative behaviour designed to bring out anyone's basest instincts. I'm not condoning that for anyone, no matter what their beliefs. It's not kind or loving, and people who do that may want to think about what's driving them. But it's also been my experience that most Christian women aren't doing that.

They are sensitive, caring and not out to lead anyone astray. How they look has very little bearing on how they behave.

It's always the quiet ones. Well, almost

In fact, when I was at school, the girl who looked the most stereotypically butter-wouldn't-melt was the one, it later turned out, that was making friends behind the bike sheds with all and sundry. I don't think anyone would have believed it to be the case.

For sure, it was the gum-chewing, blue-mascaraed (it was the eighties. It looked good once, honest), smoking, loud girls whose behaviour was most closely monitored for an assumed lack of moral fibre, but they didn't get the chance to let rip. When I look back now, several girls' faces pop into my mind – girls who had early and sometimes public sex, abortions, violent boyfriends, multiple partners – and they weren't generally exhibitionists. They didn't dress to attract attention. They were academic, well dressed, sometimes dowdy, polite, highly spoken of by teachers. Good girls.

Men (boys) weren't attracted to them for an occasional flash of flesh or subtle expressions of sexuality they could project their desires on to. It was something much more apparent and available than that.

So it has never seemed that obvious to me that outward attractiveness equals deliberate attempt to gain sexual interest. The girls with the deepest need for attention and affection, who went looking for it in the wrong places, were often girls who showed no outward signs.

Lessons in love

Growing up, we've all experienced many kinds of interactions with men, ranging from innocent and fun to possibly tragic or abusive. Respectful and disrespectful. Loving and not so loving. We all have defences in place, things that have got us from our starting place to where we are now. There's a good chance they do too. When we come into church, what should we expect to find? A place where we're not judged by appearance? A safe place where our walls can be taken down? Or a place where we need a whole new set of walls?

What about people coming from a world of normal interactions, where gender often doesn't even figure? Or if it does, there are many possible outcomes. The world out there isn't black and white. Most girls – and by girls, I mean the female species from teens onwards – coming into a church environment for the first time will find the dynamics very strange. Generally, men do not act the way they are used to.

I was recently visited by a Christian friend who is a fairly new addition to the fold, with limited experience of church. We bumped into a Christian male friend as we were walking down the street. We chatted, exchanged jokes, just general banter. And as we walked away, my friend said, with a raised eyebrow, "He *likes* you..."

Well, yeah, he does. But not romantically. We're just friends. The whole brother-sister thing. We argued the point for a while, coming to no agreement. She just couldn't believe a man could be like that. But as her visit progressed it became apparent that she struggled to see male attention, even affection, in a non-sexualised way, and she was starting to struggle to see men innocently too. She hadn't met heterosexual men who looked at women with an absence of sexual interest. Through various experiences in her life, she felt she had changed and she didn't like it. She used a biblical comparison. She spoke about one occasion when she had crossed a sexual line, before she was a Christian, and said it was like she had taken a bite from the apple, and, like Eve, her eyes were opened to everything. Her innocence had gone, and now she desperately wanted it back. She wanted to see things the way they really were, not assume there are sexual undertones in every male/female conversation.

It made me think about the culture of friendliness that can actually be alien to people experiencing it for the first time. If vulnerable people, or people whose boundaries may be very different to those of most church members, are greeted by people who want to hug them or ask them a lot about themselves, they are going to find that very strange. Even eye contact and prolonged smiling can be unsettling. They may misinterpret it. It could scare them away, as much as unfamiliar spiritual language or strange ritual.

Or it could make them think that person is interested in more than they are showing at the moment. And they may respond to that perception. Christians need to have wisdom about this, to be careful not to give incorrect impressions through completely innocent behaviour. Think about where that person is coming from and what is acceptable to them.

1x husband, unrealistically perfect model, please. Out of stock? Anything in bargain corner?

So chums of the opposite sex aside, it's apparent that negotiating the etiquette of Christian romance is an act worthy of the Brontes (and some of it possibly dates from that time too). There are contradictory expectations which can be confusing to those long established, never mind newcomers. There is an apparent norm of marrying young and reproducing lovely Godly children with biblical names and how splendid it all is, but somehow assuming that those who didn't manage to partner off by their mid-twenties (or even late teens) must be in that category of eunuchy types that get mentioned in the New Testament and let's not make it awkward and talk about them. The fact they might be sexual beings without outlet or expression for their feelings or desires... what about that?

Then the lack of real talk about sex. It's pretty much invisible, except for reverent mentions that God invented it and he thinks it's really great and look, there's even a poem in the Bible that mentions breasts and longing. So officially we know it's great, but we don't really talk about it until... well, until when?

And when it's finally all above board, and you're official and married, what about that list of things you can and can't do once you're hitched... who wrote that? Based on what?

Then the seemingly accepted norms for marriage, which sometimes look mostly like pursuing companionship rather than having real passion – or hurrying someone remotely suitable down the aisle before your urges get the better of you.

The assumptions, and these can even be preached from the pulpit, are that a lot of women want to be home makers or have part-time, unchallenging jobs and pop out babies, and men work all hours but can't put down the toilet seat and don't want to talk (or listen). Or is that just how some people present themselves at church?

And what about the lack of openness about bodies and physiology in general? One poor girl believed she was going to start having pyramids when she grew up. She had overheard some strange talk at school about blood and pain and asked her mum what was going to happen when these pyramids that everyone else seemed to be having started happening to her? Were they going to hurt? I grew up in a household that turned off the Diary of Anne Frank for being too racy because of a comment about periods. The Victorian fear and loathing of our bodies seems to still be alive and well in some parts of the church. We just don't mention it.

A bit of an eye-opener

When the world has embraced a hedonistic or experimental approach to love and relationships that seems to have permanently redefined how people interact – friends with benefits, booty calls and all that – how do we find our way through to something that neither suppresses who God made us to be nor adopts the assumptions of a world that doesn't know God that can offer us less, or even demean or exploit us?

And what about girls who've spent years within church culture and have little experience of the world outside?

When it seems like there is a lack of suitable – or, sometimes, interesting enough – men inside there is a temptation to look at what's out there. Ever ended up chasing or being chased by non-Christian men on flimsy grounds? Wondering if there can be any justification for getting involved with someone clearly heading in a different direction?

(As you might suspect, this has never been me. Ahem.) Like the young lady who took a fancy to a colleague who presented himself as a loveable rogue. She was a Christian inexperienced in matters of romance. He was the opposite on all scores. What started her off on her reckless pursuit? The fact that he gave up chocolate for Lent. Didn't give up the heavy drinking and womanising, nor bragging about them, just laid off the Kit Kats for a few weeks. Possibly not a recipe for lifelong happiness.

Pick-'n'-mix anyone?

And then there is the spectrum of dating experiences within the Christian world. As one non-Christian male friend remarked, having observed some of the strange, strained attempts at romance going on in church circles, "You wouldn't look twice at these guys if you didn't have to go out with a Christian." Sadly he had a point. It was unbelievable to his ears that his contemporaries expected a model of femininity straight out of Stepford while very little seemed to be expected of them.

One friend came back from the pre-marriage counselling she and her fiancé were taking part in before their church wedding extremely relieved that her future husband had been told by the seemingly traditional vicar that this wasn't a case of a man marrying a replacement, if younger, version of his mother: this was a partnership. They were in it fifty-fifty. "Let's see if he remembers that bit when we discuss the ironing later," she said wryly.

The notion that a good Christian wife should be passive and predominantly domestic still looms large in some circles. For non-Christians looking in, it seems bizarre. Used to equality in their relationships, no matter how much debate takes place about whose turn it is to do the washing up, it seems unusual that women's careers automatically take a back seat, if they have a career at all. Each to their own for every couple, but let's make sure all the options are on the table. And not just the immaculately laid table with the wholesome dinner on it made squeezed in between organising a jumble sale and doing the laundry for the entire household. It can all start to seem less about attraction and more about suitability. The infamous list for starters. Or just plain pragmatism. One wife-seeking man recently reviewed available options within his local church by literally debating the pros and cons of each eligible lady with no particular preference or attraction in mind. He would just go for whichever one seemed the simplest option and best fit. And who says romance is dead?

THE ONE and other distractions

And let us now turn to that elusive holy grail of Christian relationships: THE ONE. The idea that God has created just one perfect partner for each of us seems to be strangely ingrained in Christian culture. Out in the world, there are similar ideas, of course – you only have to pitch up at your local cinema to see how many buy into Cinderella notions of true love bringing strangers together (through films, that is. A cinema is not a previously unmentioned site for finding the perfect romance, before some of you rush down there). There are some whose exceptional stories of meeting seem to support the theory that God is indeed moving heaven and earth to bring together modern-day Adams and Eves, and no other would do. But it would appear that these are often that – the exception. When we meet a person and fall in love it can seem that God has created them just for us, and us for them, that no one else could ever do. Bring on the choirs of angels. To see couples totally happy together and wanting no one else is a beautiful thing. But maybe one or two of us (not you or me, obviously. I mean other people) project this desire onto people who may not be remotely suitable, but seem to be ticking those oh-so-important boxes. It isn't as rare as you might think for men and women to suddenly hear declarations of undying love, wrapped up in the fail-safe assurance that "God told me we were going to be together", from people they barely know. One woman faced this along with a marriage proposal from a man with whom her only contact was a weekly prayer hour. Should I mention it didn't end in a wedding?

It would be fair to say that conviction over someone being THE ONE, whether expressed unblinkingly to a slightly alarmed individual, more subtly amongst sympathetic friends or even as an abstract concept, usually involves a certain level of physical attraction. I have had to hide a few smiles over the years as I've been told by female friends that God has their perfect man ready and waiting somewhere out there, and he just happens to physically resemble George Clooney, Brad Pitt or whoever lights their fire in celebrity world. When I've questioned why they are so sure God doesn't have a more regular-looking guy in mind, the answer (often accompanied by a blank stare) is usually along the lines of God wanting them to be happy/the best for them/to fulfil the desires of their heart and that best just happens to come in a Hollywood-worthy package, OK? I'm not saying they can't be right, I've just noticed that not many men of any or no spiritual persuasion possess looks worthy of a movie career. There are many more who are regular, attractive or not people. Just like we are.

Beautiful people are more holy. Fact

God says he looks at our hearts. We, if we're totally honest, look at a little more. Clearly the list is not just purely made up of spiritual qualities. And the boys do it too. How much more convinced are the men I've spoken to that the women they find extremely physically attractive are the ones God has in mind for them! Like the guy who insisted the model he met through a Christian dating website was THE ONE before they had met in person (she wasn't, as it turned out).

And sadly I've lost count of the number of girls who've claimed a man as their own on the basis of a fleeting meeting, or even a glance at a photograph. The earmarked individual has no idea of their new honorary position and possibly may not even know of their admirer's existence, but I have been party to hours wasted by eager young women looking for the object of their desire on social networking sites, discussing with friends (often keenly encouraging them) and generally daydreaming. I have not so far (sorry, girls) seen these crushes come to anything. In the meantime, opportunities for real relationships, romantic or non, are passing by.

The height of romance...

So if you can get past the assumptions, take a risk and eventually get to a point where you might get to know someone in a more than passing way, what happens then? In many cases that seems to depend on what kind of church and Christian environment you're in. I lived for years in a city where the Christian community was well integrated; people met and mixed in all kinds of settings. Activism and community projects brought people together; there were grown-up activities and even dates.

Dates? Did someone just faint? Yes, dates. Where a man and a woman went by specific arrangement to a particular place with the express intention of investigating their romantic potential. This, my friend, is controversial.

There has been something of a movement within parts of the church away from dating. In some respects, that fits. With people thrown together and spending time anyway, there are opportunities to get to know someone well without making a big deal out of the process. Clare and James met in church while stacking chairs. (I know, it brought a tear to my eye too. I can't wait to see who plays them in the movie.) They became friends, spent time together. There were outings and dinner parties involving others. Clare was a great hostess anyway, brilliant at getting people together and making connections. James was a frequent guest. Then one day he stepped it up.

A mutual friend likes to claim responsibility for this, by pointing out to James that while he was updating his internet dating profile and still not meeting anyone suitable, it was possible his perfect woman was right under his nose.

How would he recognise her?

By the beautiful way she stacked chairs (OK, I made up that bit). He gave it some thought. And decided his friend might be right. So he left a plant on her doorstep, with an enigmatic note. And it went from there. Love blossomed and they are now very happily married with a baby.

But I've heard of more spontaneous beginnings. And I have even heard of many people being whisked off to well-thought-out, imaginative, exciting appointments designed to show them that someone wants them to know how much they think of them and wants them to be more than a little bit impressed too. This is no casual coffee designed to test out the list. This is stepping out to pursue.

To get to know the real person. To do something that will engage and intrigue them. To make them stop and turn aside. To break the routine. To make someone feel wanted and interesting and desirable.

Ooh, sounds a bit exciting. Is that, well, Christian?

I was going to get a butler, but if you're free...

It may be more Christian than some of the thinly veiled misogyny that passes for romance these days. Telling a woman that you're looking for a wife and expounding what you expect of that wife isn't saying much about a genuine interest in that person and what makes them tick. That unique, beautiful, amazing person God has created, just waiting to be buried under less than fulfilling expectations. If these men weren't Christians, I don't think they'd get airspace. I've heard too many laying out their requirements for a woman to be involved in certain areas of church life – usually involving child care and maybe some nice praying with a group of other ladies – but nothing that might cross with their areas of expertise (something forward-thinking and authoritative, usually), all the while keeping the house in order and dinner on the table.

And this may be impossible to prove, but it seems the less effort and originality that goes into that meeting (or phone call), the more likely it is that the person being questioned isn't particularly important to the person doing the questioning. And the less likely that any kind of friendship will develop if romance doesn't.

And the girls aren't off the hook either. By assessing a man by appearance, his comparison to non-Christian counterparts, his material wealth and possessions, thus subconsciously calculating whether they can support someone, or wanting a man in a position of church leadership or authority, are we projecting our own stereotypical and limited views onto men who may have a lot of other things to offer?

Ask the mature couples you know if they are the same people now that they were when they met their partners. See how much has evolved, how their lives have developed together, how they've changed.

None of us are the perfect package. I'm not suggesting we start settling for people we don't genuinely want to be with just so that we're not alone, but I am asking if, somewhere along the way, we might have thrown a lot of other requirements into the mix that have somehow created a hybrid super-list of unassailable spirituality and all the things the world wants too. Go on, ask those happy couples you know how they started out. They may not have been the perfect match on paper they appear to be now. On a purely mischievous note, meeting people to work out if there is romantic potential can have entertainment value and open the way for a good time even if nothing further develops. An initial spark of interest can easily find itself fading out and into a fun and fulfilling friendship instead. I don't think Christian dates are more eccentric than non, but they can seem that way. Assume that each of these scenarios is overlaid with the usual expounding of The List, in one form or other...

The birds and the been theres

At least you only have to read about it. Some of us have had to go through the experience. Take the sincere and attractive man who seemed like a good bet – until he insisted on bringing his trick-performing dog on the date too. A great way to test a relationship at the outset is to see how adaptable you are to having a floppy-eared mongrel determine where you'll be eating your dinner every time you go out. And no, I don't mean the man in question. Or the man who turned up forty-five minutes late for a date he had spent weeks plucking up the courage to ask for, and then dragged his date from venue to venue looking for somewhere that wouldn't make him sweat (to be fair, there was a heat wave at the time, but it's just not a great ice breaker. Actual ice would have done the trick) and who stopped off on yet another walk across town in search of air conditioning to eat a muffin in a bus stop while his date stood awkwardly by. Offering her a bite from the half-eaten delicacy (which actually belonged to someone already standing at the bus stop – don't ask) didn't make her thankful to be there.

Or the man who took a date to the theatre and booked front-row seats without realising that the production of Singing in the Rain involved an authentic recreation of actual singing in the rain which meant everyone in the first few rows got soaked. A date that was a literal washout.

Then there are the dates that barely mask at least one participant's personal issues. I've found these are best avoided. Like the occasion an initially pleasant man spent the evening throwing out insults at the girl he had dragged away from Coronation Street with the promise of a good time. Tell that girl that you're resigned to the fact you're not going to meet the woman of your dreams or even someone you find beautiful and you're now searching simply for a companion to share the journey through life, and you may be able to salvage the moment. Tell the same girl you'd really been hoping for someone with a delicate nose but you're prepared to compromise so she shouldn't worry, and you'll be lucky if you can still see that nose or any other part of her face by the time you get to the end of the sentence.

Or the man who spent the first date trying to determine if his slim companion intended to stay that way by (not very subtly) monitoring her menu choices.

Or the man who announced on his first meeting with a potential partner that should things get to the stage of a wedding ("play your cards right") he wouldn't want to be involved in the details. He'd just like to turn up on the day, thanks.

Or the man who misjudged his date's age and, despite being several years her senior, declared himself shocked that she was a decade older than he thought, and this may impact upon his plans to reproduce many offspring, but he would be prepared to settle for less children. She was prepared to settle for bearing none of his babies – and a man who didn't care how old she was.

Let's take it slowly. Let's get married *next* week

But what if, against the odds, it all starts to fall into place? With announcements of marriage sometimes occurring before the first date is over, Christian relationships can seem to accelerate faster than their non-Christian counterparts. Is it because we have a tendency to over-share as soon as we meet? A desire not to be alone? Whether it's well-intentioned encouragement not to get involved with people if there isn't a serious chance of something significant happening, or plain old frustration, it does seem that marriage is on the cards much sooner than in many regular liaisons.

While it's commendable not to want to lead people on or pursue someone when we have no intention to commit no matter what, we need maturity in understanding how people come together and then decide if they want to stay that way. But it can get a wee bit surreal. I've heard of weddings decided from the first date – just not necessarily by both parties.

Or of people planning hen parties and appointing bridesmaids before a first date had even taken place, then being very surprised when a kiss took place at the end of it. So forward!

Or of wedding dresses secretly bought and kept in the attic in order to be fully prepared when the question was asked. Thankfully the unsuspecting man didn't sense an excess of lace and panic. And thankfully he did eventually ask.

Or of advance warning issued to housemate that when engagement was announced (this was pre any relationship actually starting) they were on countdown to find alternative accommodation as the wedding would be going ahead within one month. No hanging about. As it happened the housemate got a better offer first, and managed to get to the altar in three months. Still pretty impressive.

A happy ending

Let's return to Clare and James for a moment. When they thought there was a good chance they wanted to stay together, rather than rush in they proceeded with caution. Convinced that they wanted to marry each other, they booked themselves in for pre-engagement preparation. Not the traditionally accepted marriage preparation that takes place before the ceremony just to make sure people know what they're getting themselves into. No, this was a different thing altogether. It was surprising, and to my ears not very romantic. I was intrigued. And I began to ask around. Single people looked surprised (maybe they were just surprised to hear that anyone was getting married). Couples were interested. It hadn't been around when they'd been at that stage. They had floated along on a cloud of conviction that eternal bliss was theirs for the taking and were still working it through. It wasn't until I mentioned it to two specific groups of people that their emphatic responses made me rethink my lack of enthusiasm.

Category one, the minister. A man who had taken more weddings than he could remember said it should be compulsory for couples the minute, if not the second, marriage was a feasible opportunity. Once the question is popped, he said, the rollercoaster has begun. The path is set. The co-ordinates are decided. The course is mapped out (you get the picture). There is then no impartial questioning. A public commitment has already been made. Emotions are high. The momentum is unstoppable. Doubts are dismissed as nerves. The earlier the idea of marriage raises its head in a relationship, the less likely it is that the couple will actually have a clue what the other one is picturing when they talk of a life together. Values, expectations, lifestyle, finances and the vast amount of variables that falls under the neat heading "Everything Else" are all parked under a big question mark to be dealt with once the ceremony is over.

Category two, the divorced. Sue rolled her eyes and said simply, "I wish. It would have saved so much heartache."

So where does that leave us? Walking a fine line of openness without over-sharing. Somehow having our feet on the ground even as we're being swept off them. Working through our own issues so that we're not forced to hide our real selves or expect anyone else to fix the problems. Getting to a place of realising that no one is perfect, not even us.

Let's be charitable and assume they're *trying* to help

And what if after all that you don't meet anyone, never mind THE ONE? When it becomes tedious, infinitely explaining singleness to non-Christian friends who don't understand why you don't just get stuck in. Who may take matters into their own hands by organising seating at their wedding so you're placed next to the only single man on the guest list and tip him off in advance so he has his best lines prepared ("I can read you so well I can even guess what you're having for dinner..." It's a wedding reception;

we're all having the same thing). Is it bearable, especially if the only other single females in the room are not there with a view to meeting a man: the nanny, the wedding planner and the lesbian? (What a day that was.)

Or your friends buy you an action man figure for your birthday so at least you're not alone.

Or your friends write lonely hearts ads as a birthday present. No really, you shouldn't have...

I can remember times when it seemed everyone had it going on except me. Why? Because I wanted a man who had the same beliefs and hadn't met one who would have been a good fit.

Always the bridesmaid. Sometimes the old maid...

So how do you work through the fact that your friends have all moved on and you haven't? That their priorities have shifted to relationships, marriage, babies and up-sizing, and you don't have anything new going on? When the weekend comes around and, apart from turning up to church on Sunday, you don't have anything planned? Once, trying to celebrate a long-awaited promotion, it turned out that my friends were only free on a Monday night. Their weekends were suddenly full of partners and romance. And they wouldn't be there till late because of work, and would have to leave early because of work the next day.

And doesn't that just add to the sadness of it all somehow? That work, the thing people allegedly eschew on their deathbeds as having stolen all their time, the thing we're only meant to do in order to have all the other, real, things in life, is the only thing that's got anything going on. And slipping down people's priority list too. When they're still the most important people in your life, but they've moved on, it can be a really sad time. Who do you go on holiday with? Spend your free time with? Do you just become an expert gooseberry? I've lost count of the number of evenings spent on friends' sofas, while the happy couple curl up (they don't go out any more), want to know what's new out there (again, they don't go out any more), wonder if you've seen any mutual friends (because they don't go... you get the picture). When did you become their personal society correspondent, living it up so they don't have to? Probably not the greatest way to spend a weekend.

Single and ready to mingle...

And try explaining to those non-Christian friends why this is the way it is. Sceptical is an understatement. The questioners don't beat around the bush. So you still haven't met anyone? Why do you have to wait to meet a Christian? What if God just wants you to have a nice time and forget about being good for a while? Don't you want to have sex?

Their intentions are good, but when the answers don't change year after year, it can be easy to fall into the category of Single, with all that entails. And then what? How is it possible to work through a life that seems to be going in the opposite direction of most people you know so that you're not left up Lonely Creek in a leaky canoe?

By redefining. Denise had the same three female best friends for years. They had always done everything together. Except meet people. As the other girls eventually met and married nice boys, Denise didn't. But she still spent all her social time with them. Every Saturday night, now with partners in tow, they would have dinner. Spend cosy evenings as a neat seven-some. She hadn't branched out to make any new friends and she was more and more frustrated with her situation.

By not moaning about it. Paula used to spend so much time complaining about the lack of a man in her life that her conversation consisted of little else. What was she going to talk about when she actually met someone? And how could he, a mere humanoid, possibly fill such a void? Why was she letting the walls close in on her in that way?

By relaxing. I know, so much more easily said than done. But being on constant high alert isn't going to change things. Except your stress levels. And not for the better. I've never yet met a woman who has made her dream man materialise by screeching, "WHEN?! WHEN is it going to be me?" I mean, try by all means, and let me know if it happens. If it's a case of sheer persistence I know some who may be very close to making it happen by now and I'm sure the encouragement would be appreciated.

By being brave. Don't wait for someone else to be available. Go places on your own. Not in a strident, efficient way that makes it more of a mission than a leisure activity: just step out and find things you like to do and do them. Go to the cinema, art gallery, walking, things that don't need another person in order to make them feel right. People can be very unimaginative. It often happens that when they hear about someone going somewhere they invite themselves along. Like Claudia, who organised a ball just for the fun of it. After putting the word out people jumped at the chance to dress up and dance the night away. After a while it won't seem like bravery anyway. You'll just be used to enjoying yourself, and it'll become a great habit you won't want to break.

By enjoying the time you have. Not in the way a former pastor of mine put it to me, "You must have so much time to read the Bible and pray. Hours all alone. What a joy." Er, yeah, my thoughts exactly. (Though he was the father of eight children so there may have been just a touch of envy creeping in.) I mean more along the lines of appreciating the lack of responsibility. The fact that you can eat what you want, go to bed when you want, don't have to clean up after anyone else, or explain yourself to someone. You are free! I'm not saying it doesn't get lonely. I'm just saying enjoy being by yourself.

By reaching out. I can almost guarantee that no matter how bad you feel, you will know someone who feels worse. Or someone who has just moved into the area. Or someone who seems a bit withdrawn and shy. Or a group that needs your support or time. Park your own desires for a while and get on with helping other people. It can be tremendously fulfilling, not to mention broadening your social circle, interests, experience and opening up new opportunities. And I don't mention the following story to create an ulterior motive in your mind (I know, I know, you're far too good for that) but one man, who has been happily married for years, talks of how he heard about his future wife long before he met her, because of her generosity. Through a wide circle of mutual acquaintances, the nice things she had done for people and the groups she had helped, were talked about time and again. He felt like he already knew her. "I've got to meet this woman," he thought. He did. And he married her.

By getting perspective. Not having a partner isn't the end of the world. It really isn't. God really does know our situations and how we feel about them. He doesn't share the views of some out there who make people feel second class because they don't come as part of a double act. Whatever stage you're at, he knows. And he's there with you. Hard to grasp and harder to respond to, I know, but worth contemplating. You're not alone. He loves you too much for that.

2. Flee temptation. Don't take it on holiday to a romantic honeymoon destination and hope for the best

Ah, the thrill of temptation. Don't you just love it? The tantalising tingle, the stolen glance, the shiver of excitement. Innocent fun, really. Harmless. A small indulgence. A little bit of what you fancy does you good, or so I've been told. Or maybe I was telling myself. Repeatedly.

Though is there often another feeling, somewhere in the back of my mind? Fighting for airspace amid the flurry of desire and excitement. Hastily pushed aside and ignored. A tiny little warning bell, suggesting that maybe this should be left well alone. A niggling notion somewhere deep down where you know, just know, that pursuit of this object of your desire isn't going to end well. The dictionary definitions of temptation should give the game away: "Something that seduces or has the quality to seduce; enticement;

forbidden fruit; bait; come-on; snare: lure; solicitation; the desire to have or do something that you know you should avoid".

That should spell it out, really. A flashing neon sign warning us that we are heading, speeding probably, into a dangerous area, brakes off, all warnings ignored. This isn't about addiction — probably. Nor is it about the innocent fancies and desires we often refer to as temptations these days. Muffins? Chocolate? Who are we kidding? They barely register on the temptation Richter scale. Though I'm not immune to little distractions. Perfume has the seductive power to draw me in and cause me to unwisely part with my hard-earned cash, ever since my gran bestowed a bottle of her expensive French scent on me as a wide-eyed, impressionable child. Oh the glamour. Apparently (another dubious family legend. I can't believe I'd ever be so sneaky) I used to be so bedazzled by the pretty bottles as I was wheeled around Woolworth's as a small munchkin that it wasn't until my mum was ferrying us home that my stash of scented booty would be discovered under the pushchair canopy. Don't try it — it really does only work for toddlers (or so the police told me last time...).

But the emotion didn't wear off, even if habit of petty theft did. I still love getting caught up in a fragrant fantasy — the scent, the bottle, the advertising, the art of it all. I want to say: I can't resist, I was hooked, I couldn't help myself (it doesn't stand up in court though). The things we indulge ourselves with, roll our eyes later, with a cheeky smile, and say we couldn't stop. I had to have it, we tell ourselves and our friends.

So is it totally harmless? There's probably no major damage if we know when to stop (ideally before becoming acquainted with the inside of a cell) or we're not using distractions to avoid an inner emptiness. This is about those things that don't fit into that category. Those areas of weakness which go beyond harmless.

Things that we know, as the dictionary suggests, we should avoid. Things that hurt us, and maybe others. Things that may steal our direction and destiny. Things that may even destroy us. I'm not talking about addiction. I don't mean the spiral of hard drugs or alcohol or anything else that can wreck our minds and bodies. I'm talking about the emotions that surround our areas of weakness and what we do when faced with something we really want but that we really shouldn't have. Anyone? OK, just me then. I will try to take my own advice for a change.

How not to be silly

Do we have to learn the hard way? Probably not, but when we do it's probably because we've already ignored the easy ways. Did I say we? I'm speaking only for myself, of course. Hands up, I admit it. From past experience, slow to spot the danger signs and slower still to turn and run. I'm sure that's just me though. You're wise and knowing, nodding sagely at this and reflecting on how every decision you've made has edified and benefited your life and the lives of all around you. How strong you are, how heavenly minded, or at least filled to bursting with common sense. You'd never turn a blind eye to such foolishness and walk, nay charge, headlong in.

You are above all that, aren't you? Aren't you...? Didn't Oscar Wilde have a point though? Or was that just for me?

My proud notion that self-control was high on the list of my many virtues took a while to crumble, with the slow dawning of the fact that my self-control was indeed impeccable, unimpeachable and rock solid – just with one small condition. It was all of those things only when I really wasn't that bothered about the thing on offer. Cigarettes? Not for me. Getting drunk? Not bothered (well, not for years anyway). Drugs? Never been interested. Tattoos? Don't see the point. That lovely, must-have top winking at me from the window of Top Shop? Not this month.

So what did that actually mean? The difference between me and the people around me who just couldn't say no to these things wasn't that I was stronger than them. The difference was that I wasn't actually tempted. I didn't really want them. They had no pull on me. While it felt to those around me that I was in a permanent state of self-denial, as they became high, merry or elaborately illustrated with Chinese symbols, ickle daisies and dolphins, I wasn't really resisting anything. I just didn't have the same areas of weakness.

Our temptations are not all the same. It was no challenge to resist things that I wasn't drawn to; I only noticed that they seemed to have a pull on everyone else. Years were spent in a state of idle speculation about why the most blatant of life's temptations had little appeal to me. Apart from the occasional glass of pinotage, I could take or leave most vices. But I was severely mistaken. Dear old Oscar had a major moment of self-awareness when he announced he could resist everything except temptation. As it turns out, Oscar and I had that in common.

So what happened when I was actually tempted?

Meltdown

Not straight away, of course. Temptation is generally a slippery slope. Maybe a slow moving one, but once you're on, it's hard to get off. There is good reason that the Bible tells us to flee temptation. Even Jesus, in the only prayer he suggested we use, includes a specific request not to be led into it. Why? I'm guessing that he, knowing us inside out, knew what the consequences would be. Nowhere does God or good sense suggest that we try and stick it out. Face temptation, my child. Keep staring at that thing you want that you shouldn't have. It'll do you the world of good, build character, toughen you up.

Nope. Well, not in my version anyway (and I've tried a few. There really is no get-out clause). So I suppose if I've learned anything, what's key to all of this is recognising temptation. Well surely, you say, that's easy: it's probably a long list of everything you want and know you shouldn't have. That may be true to a point. But I surrounded myself for years with the things that everyone wanted and wasn't tempted. I didn't realise what an individual thing it was. Temptation wasn't high on my list of priorities. I wasn't looking for it, hadn't really felt it and wasn't ready to flee it. I didn't know what it was, because none of those things were my temptations. I'm not encouraging anyone to think long and hard about all the things they want that are out of reach. Not unless you want to end up miserable and pining. What I'm suggesting is simply to learn to recognise the feelings that arise when you enter a danger area and the red light comes on in your head. Only you know when that's happened and only you can decide what happens next.

Magnificent obsession

Let's use smoking as an example, a metaphor, if you will. I've had friends who loved to smoke. With a deep and abiding passion. Who woke up regularly in the night, groping around for a packet, as their bodies craved nicotine. Who would walk through blizzards in their night clothes to buy cigarettes. Who would shake their car mats over a cigarette paper to catch any fallen tobacco that may have come loose from earlier smokes. Who would excuse themselves from any social situation to spend five minutes alone with their skinny white friend (not me, the cigarette). And who eventually, as life, age, children and health intruded, reluctantly gave up their true love. So I have this on good authority. The temptation to smoke is still there. You're minding your own business, haven't thought about smoking in months. After all, can't smoke in pubs or restaurants any more. Or on trains or buses. Or hotels. Or anywhere the ex-smoker may find themselves at a weak moment. It's not a temptation any more. It doesn't even cross your mind. You feel better, look better and smell better. You have more money. You're friends with your lungs again. You don't miss it; it was just something you used to do.

Until... one night, as you're leaving a film with friends, someone near you lights up. The smell hits your nostrils. In a flash, you're back there. Everything you ever loved in one huge, intoxicating breath. You're having the whole experience again in technicolor smell-o-vision. All your senses are caught up; the rest of the world is a blur. Why did you ever deny yourself this? Surely no reason is good enough? And now you want to smoke.

And that's how I've learned to recognise temptation.

Acceleration and intensity.

Months, even years, can pass without anything to trigger it. There can be things that would once have tempted me that now no longer have any effect. Like some ex-smokers who say, years later, that the smell has no pull on them, no draw at all, that they have no desire to go back, that they have truly left it behind. And that can happen.

But this is about what happens when desire is suddenly there again. When it happens – the rush, the speed, the blocking out of rational thought, the vivid mental images and fantasy are there in a flash.

Suddenly, it's all different, the world has shifted on its axis and the seed is planted. Temptation is back.

Wherefore art thou...

So, what finally tempted me over the edge? Well, I won't pretend I'm not drawn by at least some of the same basic clichés as everyone else. You won't find me on one of those late-night documentaries trying to marry a tree or a farm animal. I am far from unique. I give in to the "temptations" of cake, chocolate, desserts, puddings and Radiohead like many sane people. I also have an appreciation, shall we say, for an attractive man. "Well, who doesn't?" you're shouting back in disbelief. "Is that it?" Yes, in some ways, that's it. I'm a woman who appreciates the simple charms of masculinity. Not all of them, of course. I grew up with a brother, and was surrounded by his friends from my earliest recollections. There's no mystery or enigmatic allure or romanticising about the male species from thereon in. Believe me. Still a few flashbacks that can induce shuddering moments and silent weeping. I've had close male friends for years. I've had great connections with lots of male colleagues. And there has been no interest on my part in anything more than normal everyday relationships with them. No attraction, no nothing.

But occasionally – very, very occasionally – I would come into contact with someone more intriguing. More than just a passing observation, more of a chemical reaction. Thankfully, and very mercifully, this has only happened to me once in a blue moon. A handful of times in my whole life. And a small handful at that. Almost every man I've ever met has had absolutely no effect on me (despite what they might have thought). I'm not talking about a compulsion or obsession here. This is not about addiction. But when I've suddenly had that moment, when I've looked at or spoken to or interacted with a man I find attractive at a whole other level, it's like the smoker getting the unexpected blast of intoxication. Acceleration and intensity. Unlikely to be visible to anyone else, but I've just found myself on the road to temptation. The question now is what do I do with that?

Along came a boy

Let me tell you about the last time this happened to me and what I learned along the way. Once upon a regular evening, at a friend's party, I met a man. This may seem a little harsh now, but I couldn't understand the fuss that was being made in my social circle over his so-called good looks and general attractiveness. I just didn't get it. There was no instant chemistry, no instant anything. He was just a bloke, a boy really (not legally a boy. Far from it. We're not heading into dubious territory, don't worry). But he was new in town and started hanging out with us a lot. We sat in the park, we ate and drank, we walked. He invited me on a group holiday that summer, with people I knew better than I knew him. I accepted. Why not? There was lots of chatting and laughing. I still thought he was a little silly and a bit socially clumsy, but with more affection than before, and I had finally noticed the physical charms that were frequently pointed out by others.

One unexpectedly warm and sunny day, we all lay in the park, argued over the crossword, walked by the river and I can remember turning to look at him and suddenly there was the blast. I hadn't looked at his face, I had suddenly glanced at his body and the rush had happened. I looked away, of course, but that was the trigger. The image was planted, the hormones arrived with a fanfare and that was that.

Quick disclaimer: let me just reiterate, this isn't a regular thing for me. I don't struggle with this issue on a daily basis, crazed with lust wherever I turn, and I don't have this reaction to the vast, vast majority of men I encounter, nor do I steal glances at their bodies or any other part of them. Please be reassured. Your male companions are quite safe. This was different. It had been years since I had felt this kind of temptation; I had forgotten how bewitching it was, how quickly I could get drawn in. And I had already arranged to go on holiday with it.

I consulted friends, almost jokingly. I had no reason to think he was interested in me at all. There had been no sign, and I wasn't expecting there to be. It was a chemical reaction, I reasoned. We were friends, and that was that. I just had to get over it. I didn't flirt or make any advances. Not even in that subtle, pouty, hair-twirling way some of us may use to make our interest known or to test the water for reciprocation (no, not you, of course. You'd never do that). He was single and looking for love. I was single and actively not, well, not in his direction. He had no reason to suspect. I didn't think he'd be interested even if he did. So, on that level I thought I was safe.

The only issue was my own feelings. And the rush of them has only one natural conclusion: the desire to see them fulfilled, despite all rational arguments to the contrary. This was definitely not a conscious desire though; there was no formation of strategy. I planned for it all to stay in my head. We continued to spend time together, getting ready for the holiday, occasionally just the two of us, but usually not. Shortly before we were due to fly off we had a night out at the theatre. We had talked, much as always, and then we had gone home. He had paused, looked intense for a moment, as we said goodbye, but I had put this down to his general awkwardness and thought nothing more of it.

While still debating with myself, friends and God whether I should go on the holiday, simply for the sake of my own mental purity, certain things had popped into my mind. One was the random but very distinct image of blinds closing. I knew this was me closing my mind to what I was heading into, but I still carried on. Another was a TV theme tune, Midsomer Murders, which had burst into my head – I didn't even recognise it without investigation. I knew this was a strong indication that someone (me) was blithely heading towards a kind of sorry ending that summer. It only just crossed my mind as I sit here writing this, years later, that midsummer's day was actually during the holiday. I knew from years of experience that God was speaking to me, and despite everything I was still rationalising my reasons for going.

With my insincere pondering on those revelations causing me only a moment's hesitation, I packed and prepared to go. I was convinced that the man in question was not interested in me, that we wouldn't be alone anyway, and I actually rehearsed how I would say no if for some insane reason he tried to kiss me. I was truly blinded and, on some level, loving it. I thought I had it all under control.

That illusion lasted almost to the end of the first day. After arriving in what turned out to be a beautiful and idyllic honeymoon destination (but of course. Would it all have happened in rainy Butlins?) and not having had any sleep in nearly twenty-four hours, I fell asleep on him in a taxi and his response was more than that of a friend. Despite telling a mutual friend over breakfast the next day that nothing was going to happen, and meaning it, things unfolded from there. Quickly.

By the time we flew back, we had had more starry-eyed moments than a rom com box set. We had been like love-struck teenagers. In that way it was quite innocent, holding hands, kissing and cuddling, staring into each other's eyes all the time. Over dinner. By the pool. At every ancient ruin in a twenty-mile radius. Even in the airport. It was intoxicating. Undoubtedly not for the mutual friend who found themselves the unfortunate gooseberry, but so caught up were we that this selfishness didn't really register. I can only imagine we were an absolute nightmare to be around.When we arrived home, we met again the next day. Even away from the paradise surroundings, it felt the same. But it was then that I told him that it couldn't carry on. That we wanted different things, that it wouldn't work. That it was never going to come to anything.

When I headed back to church the week after I was in a sorry state. Slipping quietly through the big wooden door, I found my way to the back, slid into an empty row and cried. Cried throughout the service, from start to finish. Thank God that church was a loving, compassionate and solid place, not fazed by emotion or distress. Someone moved from their seat to sit with me, and held me without saying a word. I cried some more. At the end of the meeting I didn't hang around to chat. I made my excuses and slipped back out of the door. I hadn't made it more than a few steps when I was lovingly apprehended by the pastor's wife. A choked version of the sad story was blurted out to her and she listened with understanding and without judgement. Her advice was simple: to think fully about the consequences of choosing a life with a man on a different path and the heartbreak and lack of full satisfaction that would bring.

Her advice was good, but unnecessary. I had known what my decision would be from the outset. Before anything had started, from the first flicker of lust, I had known. I had known during the whole of the holiday, from when I had got so tired that I had fallen asleep on his shoulder and been distantly but distinctly aware as I drifted off, of how he had responded. I had known before he first kissed me. Before I even knew he wanted to. That night after the theatre before we had even left the country, when he later admitted he had wanted to kiss me but hadn't. Throughout every moment we were together.

There was a tug of war, tug of love, whatever you'd call two people torn over a situation where, despite no rational reason for one of them and despite mutual feelings, they can't be together. Persuasion of all sorts, to try and move someone to the thing they desperately want. Urges to give in, to succumb, to feel. Hurt at why someone would let them get involved knowing all along they wouldn't be together. This is like Romeo and Juliet, he said one day, when we were both worn out with the wrangling and debate. And we all know what happened to them.

The heartbreak went on and on. I cried every day for a month. I did very little else. I can attribute one large, specific wrinkle to that month of weeping. My face was permanently creased with pain. A pointless burst of vanity approximately three weeks into Tear-Fest led to several days of flattening the wrinkle with both hands every time I cried, in a last-ditch attempt not to degenerate completely. I was wrecked. Unable to stop the gut-wrenching sobs. Empty of everything except thoughts of what I had lost. There was no distraction and no respite from my unhappiness. Bless those kind friends who tried to help, distract me, took me places, watched me cry and did what they could.

Weeks later, back in church, I sat alone in the long wooden row, still sad beyond words. The pastor's lovely wife approached, smiled sadly and touched my shoulder. "Yes, God is merciful," she said and nodded. Somewhere in my clouded brain, amid the tears, that word registered. Merciful? For letting me go through this?! For not removing the object of my fascination and downfall from view before any of this had ever started? Or removing me from him? Or at least rendering him deeply unattractive? For not warning me in a dream to stay well away? For not filling my head with scriptures instead of images of romance? For not stopping me from getting on a plane and flying off into an irresistible concoction of hormones, moonlight and deserted beaches?

Yes, merciful. Because this wasn't the first time. I had been there before. Only a few years before I had run headlong into an unwise dalliance. This time no accident. And God had warned me vividly in a dream. And filled my head with verses and songs. And I had done it anyway. And ended it in very similar circumstances. And I had cried. And others had been hurt. I had felt that awful emptiness and I had promised myself that I would not put myself in that situation again. That I had learned my lesson.

But I hadn't learned something very important. That temptation isn't about disobedience. That it will come along regardless of our resolution. Though my intention had remained, I hadn't seen this coming. The decision to wait until I met someone who God introduced into my life was still strong. I had clung to the notion that friendship could be maintained even if I found someone incredibly tempting, because I knew it couldn't go anywhere long term, and I was past getting involved in the short term. Especially if that person was far removed from the picture of the ideal I had built up.

I had done lots of things right. I had acknowledged the attraction to friends I was accountable to, who knew me well, but I hadn't taken it seriously. Those friends who had been around the world and knew the lay of the land were not convinced, despite my humorous assurances. The dubious looks over dinner, when I assured them that a sun-soaked holiday with a gorgeous but unsuitable man I was blushing and giggly over would not cause any problems. They couldn't stop me, but they did what they could. Interestingly some Christian friends had a considerably more romantic take on events both before and after – that maybe this was God at work, that we had all become Christians at some point and why wouldn't this be his time? That maybe he was put there by God and I should see what happened. Thankfully I can't summon up now the intensity with which I wished this could be true, and it certainly isn't the case now. How fervently I hoped, despite knowing how unsuitable he was, that God could make a way, and that we could be together. I don't feel good about the fact that the destiny and vision God had laid out and planned so lovingly for me was hanging by a thread at that time. Despite knowing that pursuing the relationship would be costly in so many ways, and would probably have drained me of everything good, there were moments, despite my intention, that I would have done anything. I am extremely grateful that these feelings are long gone.

Some non-Christian friends were confused by events. They just didn't see what the problem was. Why not just have a bit of fun? Maybe God's sent him along as a stopgap, someone to spend a bit of time with just for now. Why does everything have to be permanent? Why does it matter if you don't believe the same things? If you have everything else in common, isn't that enough? My partner and I don't share the same views on everything, but that makes things more interesting. Just sleep with him – why not? They weren't on the same page as me, but I understood why it seemed so alien to them. Many were in happy, loving relationships. They wanted me to be happy too. Self-denial had never been a part of their recipe for happiness. If it was right in front of you, and was going to feel good, go for it!

They tried their best to understand that I really believed God had a better plan, even though that understanding filtered through looks of utter confusion. That he didn't want me to veer off for temporary distractions, to satisfy urges. Not because he was an unsympathetic killjoy, but because he could see ahead of me, and them, to a conclusion that would work out much better than the one I was scrabbling around with, trying to make fit. Self-denial now was for greater satisfaction later. You may hear single Christian women talking about how their man will be worth the temporary frustrations and when he finally comes along, nothing could be better. Confidence indeed.

One naughty friend used to say to me, starting a pep talk designed to inspire hope for the future, "You just wait, people will be staring. It'll be great. They won't believe that after so long you've ended with up with someone so...smelly. World record holder for unpleasant bodily functions. Face to match."

Thanks. I really can't wait.

20/20 hindsight is a marvellous thing

In the natural world, we are careful to avoid areas of weakness and encourage others to do the same. A disused mine or decaying bridge would be highlighted, marked out as a potentially dangerous area, with whatever precautions were necessary to avoid disaster. My area of weakness was identified but not clearly marked out with the emotional equivalent of warning signs, barbed wire, electric fences, and over time I grew complacent. I got used to the uneven ground, the slipperiness and uncertainty, and became careless. I hadn't forgotten how much it had hurt last time I had ventured into the danger area and fallen, but I felt I knew the ground much better now, could navigate it and remain upright. This self-deception was exposed for the lie that it was, and more people than me got hurt. The key thing was the thing I hadn't done. I hadn't fled. Dramatic language? Maybe, but anything less wasn't going to cut it.

Running had to mean really running and not looking back, not making it about the chase.

There's a great old quote which sums up the sneaky urge to see what happens: "Those who flee temptation generally leave a forwarding address." It's not about playing hard to get, it's about being impossible to get because you've run for your life.

So have I changed? Yes and no. I know that I'm not meant to be strong enough to put myself in the middle of avoidable temptations and resist them. I'm not sure anyone is. I haven't developed a magical immunity. God tells us to flee for good reason. And if we can't, and only then, he gives us what we need to resist. All this I know and vividly understand. I hope now that when faced again with the rush of intoxication I will respond differently. I hope that it will be toward the man God has brought into my life for the right reason, and not pretty but forbidden fruit, but if not, I will know to flee.

Oh man, I pray that I will do that. That the sudden rush won't take me so much by surprise that I find myself wandering, mentally or otherwise. Our judgement can be severely impaired when temptation is given free reign. I was once told by a friend considering leaving her husband for another man that she just didn't know what God wanted her to do. She'd been praying and hoping that he would give her a direction, but to no avail. She was, she said with great sincerity, really, really stuck. If only God would give her some kind of answer. Hmm, tricky.

God spoke to me even recently of the importance of managing every thought (I've noticed God does that once you start getting to know him. It's almost like he cares). It is exceptionally easy to fall into wishful thinking and not even be aware we're doing it. The tiniest thoughts can take root and we will feed them without realising we are doing so. All of these things start in the mind.

With the fertile soils of our imagination ready and waiting for fresh stimulation we need to choose carefully which way we will go.

Rebel rebel

But there was also something else going on. Something was at the root of me not resisting temptation. Rebellion. I wasn't happy with what God had given me and I wanted something else. Finding myself single for several years after returning to God following a decade away from him, and having ended the relationship I was in at that time, I had expected more than I had now got. The milestones of meeting the perfect man I had set (in consultation with no higher power, I freely admit) had passed unfulfilled. I was bored and frustrated. I wanted fun and romance. So I took it.

This fundamental unhappiness with where I was at in life was a time bomb. Despite knowing that God had plans for my life I didn't like where I was at that moment. I think that often all the things we do in vain to change our situations are a sign that we've lost touch with God, even if it's not noticeable to the outside world. Even back in Bible days, when King David resorted to murder to cover up for the fact he had made another man's wife pregnant and was finally confronted with his crime (he too was perhaps ignoring the temptation warning signs just a little), he realised that his biggest crime was actually against God.

Somewhere along the way he had given himself over to temptation and seen it through to fulfilment, no matter that the consequences were so severe. And in doing that, at the most fundamental level, he had expressed dissatisfaction with what God had given him and expressed it by taking something God hadn't given him. The means and the method were secondary, in some ways. What mattered most was that he had rebelled against God. It took me longer to reach that understanding. Even after it was all over, the attitude that I had made a huge sacrifice and "given up" was prevalent. That somehow my strength had seen me lay down that which I had most wanted. Was I expecting God to be grateful? He hadn't put me in that situation. I had packed my bag, picked up my passport and headed there myself. Thrown myself into a situation that, even if unrequited, was still not honourable to anyone involved.

Cry me a stream, at least

And then there was the disproportionate response. A month of despair for a fleeting romantic interlude? He was cute, but not that cute. My unhappiness was greater than the sum of its parts. It wasn't just about the boy, it was about more than that. About getting to a point where I had to be happy with what God was doing. What were my options from then on? To repeat the pattern? To continue to rant, cry and self-destruct? To blame someone or something else?

Thankfully I didn't dwell long in denial. God didn't want me hanging around there either. Thus far I haven't found myself in any similar mess. I hope that the combination of experience, regret, boredom with pointless relationships and knowing God better has steered me down a much more positive path. Learning to recognise the danger signs in future is still important though, as much as the resolution to avoid them. We owe it to ourselves to see it through. Good, open friendships help a lot with that. Not because we should be in a permanent state of confession and contrition, but because people who know us well can help us through, remind us where we're going and what we've got to lose.

How easy is it to passionately swear that we've learned our lesson and then, before we're even aware, as a Ms B. Spears said, oops I did it again. What if at the root of our slip-up isn't anger or rebellion but something closer to severe lack of wisdom or even carelessness? I was once in a meeting that taught about appropriate behaviour at church (always a great way to spend an afternoon). Not for the casual visitor, but for those in positions of authority, those who may need to counsel or pray for the sad, weary or distressed. A story was used to illustrate how good intentions may have negative consequences.

It was a dark and stormy night...

No, not that story. A newly divorced man had asked a single woman to pray for him to have the gift of tongues and the laying on of hands (check the Bible, it's all above board despite the terminology, you oh so worldly minded ones). She had happily agreed and taken him home to carry out the request. Somewhere in the praying, other factors had arisen and they had ended up in bed. See, said the teacher to us humble students, see how he asked for one thing and ended up getting another? Hmm, muttered the person next to me, sounds like he got exactly what he asked for. Tongues and hands a go-go. Maybe they just had different definitions in mind at the request stage. Or maybe they hadn't acknowledged that temptation may have been lurking somewhere below the surface.

I don't think the world is much like God wants it to be at the moment, and we may never be free of things that tempt us. Possibly quite the opposite. The devil is a matchmaker, as a wise person once said. The Bible, pulling no punches, says he is a ravenous wolf who prowls around looking for those he can devour. Cheerful, eh? He wants to destroy us simply because he wants to hurt God. The pleasures that come our way through him could well be there to spoil our futures. Not necessarily through tragedy, death or disease, though all of those are possible, but simply to separate us from our father. The one who created us in his own image. To deny God what he most wants: to know each one of us. OK, sermon over.

Happy endings

I know of many living happy, flourishing lives who have moved away completely from the things that used to have a hold on them. Those things are behind them, dead to them, and they really believe they cannot be touched by them any more. I want to leave you with encouragement and hope regarding temptation: that you will not always be looking over your shoulder for the things that have previously brought you down. That you will live a fulfilled life, not feeling anxious or afraid, but with peace and wisdom. That you can be an encouragement and an honest voice to those around you who may still struggle. That there are ways through. God never allows us to be tempted more than we can cope with, no matter how it seems. If the battle feels too much, it isn't. He has already worked out a way through.

Don't cut yourself off when you're tempted. Tell someone you trust what's going on. Be accountable. And when someone is accountable to you, be the voice of kindness and wisdom to them. We are all in it together. Not to judge, but to support and encourage each other to be the people we were created to be. It's important to remember that what you are going through isn't a unique problem. It's ages old. A man called Paul (check your Bible again) wrote about his frustration that he knew what he wanted to do, and yet somehow he found himself doing the opposite. What we need to be is real with each other. Don't pretend it doesn't happen to you if it does. Don't be shocked if it's happening to someone you know, even if it's a situation that you can't imagine being in. Don't judge and don't condemn. Understand why. Help and support. The Bible is very clear about how we should stand alongside people who go through things like this; it appears to be the church that can struggle with it. It could be any one of us, no matter what we think.

Be the friend you want to have

Thanks to Gandhi for the original inspiration, but you know what I mean. I can remember talking with a Christian friend about a silly situation I had found myself in, years ago. They had asked repeatedly what was going on in my life and, despite not usually confiding in them, I had told them. It was hard to do, but I thought it was best to be honest, that maybe our friendship would be better for it. Not in this case, as it turned out. They sat unemotionally throughout the sorry tale. When I finished, they stared blankly a moment longer, then shrugged, said that I'd brought it on myself and changed the subject. It was true, I had brought it on myself. But it wasn't helpful, or kind, or loving to respond in that way. Would I go to them again if I found myself in a difficult situation? No. I never spoke openly to them again, about my life or theirs. Which leaves two areas unresolved.

What if you are the person who needs to talk and you fear a similar response? Being shut down, ignored or dismissed isn't nice. If it's ever happened to you and it has scared you off ever opening up again, please reconsider. Choose carefully who you talk to. Cultivate relationships with people who speak your language.

Get to know people who are open and honest no matter what the situation, and who will speak considered wisdom into your life. Don't despair if there don't appear to be people around on your wavelength. God doesn't want you to be alone, and he hasn't brought you this far to be isolated. Sometimes when that happens, he wants us to turn more to him. But he also wants us to work together, to be stronger because we support each other.

What if you're the person being told about someone else's situation? Put yourself in their place. Imagine what it's going to take for them to open up. If you can't, don't ask them to tell you what's going on. On another occasion, I was asked about an element of my past. The truth wasn't terribly shocking, but it probably wasn't the experience of most Christians. The person who'd asked the question heard the answer, abruptly got up and left the building. Not just the room: the building. I stayed sitting where I was, not quite knowing what to do. I was careful about what I said to that person in future conversations, and that was the right thing. There were other people who wouldn't run away if I was honest, and they were the people I developed friendships with.

Don't judge. Don't look like you're judging. Don't ask about things you don't need to know. And don't tell people what you hear. Be a safe place for people to talk. Acceptance is what we are all seeking — whether we admit it or even know it — as we self-destruct and react against everything around us. When we've made mistakes along the way, who is helped by stony-faced disapproval? Even the Bible tells us that we should be with people in trouble, support them, restore them. Absolutely nowhere are we told we should judge. Are we reacting negatively because we fear our own reactions?

Scared of what we're capable of?

There but for the grace of God, an' all that. We are never in a position to assume that it could never be us.

Open season

And if we've done what seemed right, but somehow we've fallen foul of accepted Christian norms, what then? What if our relationships are above board but look, well, maybe a little dubious from the outside? If someone suggests our drinking habits are out of control because we're out in pubs late at night, or suspects we're promiscuous because we mix with people who are, then what? I guess there is some consolation in knowing that Jesus went through something similar. People wrecked his reputation because he didn't hide from individuals who lived their lives just getting by. They didn't avoid temptation. They probably weren't familiar with the concept of wanting things they couldn't have — they just got stuck in and did what came naturally. Grabbed at what they could get. And he didn't stay away from them. He just loved them and somehow showed them that there could be a different way. The last time I checked I wasn't on a par with Jesus (he was undoubtedly much, much kinder than me. Probably has a nicer smile too). I don't have the ability to rise above everything that I should like he did. I am utterly fallible. I was touched to see that God knows that already. How do I know? Because of something that is mentioned in the Bible. That Jesus isn't someone who "cannot sympathise with our weaknesses, but was in all points tempted as we are". All points? Really? I can think of a lot of points. Given time I could probably come up with quite a list. But after that is another thing to remember. That he put himself through all of that so he would know how we felt and he could offer us another way. Grace. And that is a whole other story...

3. Grace

It's an overused word, I think.

One that is possibly more significant than any other out there, and yet almost totally lost on us.

Our definitions are small, unintentionally superficial and almost completely miss the hugeness of what it is intended to be. I'm not going to get all theological about it, but this is something we need to get hold of because it's probably the most life-changing thing imaginable.

I will be lateral for a moment, to try and bring it to life.

I'm almost certain I will fail in putting across the magnitude of the concept.

But nothing ventured...

Are you sitting comfortably?

Let's imagine that you were given a beautiful and priceless crystal vase, and you had to hold on to it for a year. You couldn't let it out of your sight. Couldn't put it aside. Had to be aware of where it was all the time. When you worked, played, ate and slept. There was no getting away from it. And the thing was, you didn't really want to get away from it – it really was a lovely thing. Breathtaking, in fact. It was the most gorgeous item you had ever seen, and it had been given to you. You hadn't done anything to deserve it; you had just seen it, been bowled over by its beauty and, in a fit of uncharacteristic boldness, you had approached its maker and asked if you could have it, saying that you'd be willing to pay whatever they wanted, whatever the credit terms, you just had to have it. The owner couldn't hide their smile. They were delighted that you had been so affected by it. After all, it was a thing of great beauty, your response was just what they had hoped for, and they knew what it had cost to make it.

They said you could have it. And because you wanted it so much, and wanted it because you found it so beautiful, they didn't ask you for any money, or anything in exchange. They knew you would take care of it. The only condition was that you had to keep it with you, everywhere you went, for a whole year. Because it was so valuable, for one thing, and they suspected you might think less about that over time if it was out of sight and forget what it was worth, but also because they didn't want you to forget the gift they had given you. They had lots of other beautiful vases, vases they would love to give away to others who would be as affected as you had been, and they knew that if you had yours with you, more and more people would see it. You weighed up the offer. It was the loveliest thing you had ever seen. Ever since you had laid eyes on it, it was as if something had grabbed your heart. You didn't want to walk away and forget about it. You weren't even sure if you could. But to carry it everywhere with you? Everywhere? Wouldn't it get heavy? And wouldn't it risk getting broken? Would its value make you a target? Was there even a possibility you may get bored of it? That the thing that had so captured your attention might not seem so fascinating after a while, and you'd regret ever making this deal?

The owner watches as you turn over the decision in your mind. They know that what they are asking is a major thing. A commitment that will change a person's life for the foreseeable future. As they study you looking at their creation, they make a decision. They don't want you to leave it behind. They know that if you walk away without it, your life will be lacking something irreplaceable and they don't want you to miss it. They had created this thing of beauty knowing that its value, and their request, would make it a huge decision for anyone, no matter how moved by its beauty. So they speak slowly, and maybe with a touch of sadness.

"I do hope you will decide to take the vase."

As you open your mouth to explain your reservations, they continue, "I realise what I am asking of you is quite a commitment, and it would be unfair to place the burden of it on you alone. After all, until today you didn't even know this vase existed and now I'm asking you to rearrange your entire life around it."

The maker pauses, and takes a deep breath before continuing, "So if you would like to take it, I would like to offer you some help." The maker rings a bell on the counter beside them and waits. The curtain at the back of the shop moves, and from behind it comes a girl. She looks slight and young and a little unsure of why she has been summoned.

The maker speaks to her, but continues to look straight at you. "Grace, I have a job for you. You'll need to pack for a year – travel light though, you're going to have your hands full – and be ready to leave in an hour."

While the maker speaks, Grace also stares straight at you. She is almost expressionless, but you sense that she wasn't expecting this instruction and doesn't really like it, doesn't want to leave the maker. You feel awkward and want to say something, but as you open your mouth to speak, the maker cuts in, "Hurry, Grace, our friend has places to be."

The curtain sways again and Grace is gone. You feel a rising sense of discomfort. What just happened? Now you have to speak.

"Grace?" you start, falteringly. "You're sending Grace with me?"

The maker looks into your eyes. "Yes."

"But who is she? Where does she...? You're sending her with me? For a year?"

"Yes."

"But...what will...? Why? Won't she mind? What will I do with her?"

The maker smiles. "You won't need to do anything with her. Grace knows all about the vase, the value, the fragility, the care it needs, the process that has made it what it is; in fact, she knows it as well as I do, and she knows what it means to me. She will make sure nothing happens to it. It's your gift and her responsibility."

You don't know what to say. Minutes tick by while you turn over what you're getting yourself into. You look back at the vase. Should you leave now? Make your excuses? Run while the maker isn't looking? There must be other vases... Who needs a vase anyway?

Then something else occurs to you. "But won't you miss her?"

At that moment the curtain moves and Grace is there again, a small bag packed and a coat over her arm. "A kiss for your old dad before you go?" says the maker, extending his cheek towards her.

Dad? Can this get any worse? You wanted a vase and now you've got the teenage daughter of its maker as part of the bargain! The maker turns to her and smiles. It's a smile that puts the beauty of the vase into the shade. You keep looking until the maker turns back to you and continues to speak to his daughter. "Thank you, Grace."

So, this is it. The maker hands you the vase and you turn to leave the shop. He starts to speak again. "Grace will take care of herself, you don't need to worry about doing anything for her. She will be around all the time, wherever she is needed to make sure you and the vase are getting along OK. She's very quiet – you may even forget she's there, though I never have."

So you, the vase and Grace leave the shop and step out onto the street. Grace is behind you, waiting impassively to see which way you will go. Her eyes are fixed on the vase. You tuck it under your arm, and as you turn to walk up the road people look at you. You and the vase. Some stare at its beauty, some look surprised, some look almost disgusted and start to shout comments about it being old-fashioned. Old-fashioned? What are they talking about? If anything, it's ageless. Grace nudges you to keep going. As you turn the corner, someone approaches you. They want to know about the vase. Where did you get it? Who made it? What did it cost?

You tell them the story, about the maker and the gift and the deal and how you have Grace to help you, and they go excitedly down the street to the shop to speak to the maker themselves. Grace is still slightly behind you. You turn to smile at her, and see her eyes are kind but averted. She is looking at what's ahead.

You continue down the street, and within minutes someone

else approaches. They ask similar questions and you tell them the same story, but you forget to mention Grace. She is still hovering in the background; in fact, you're not really sure how much of a help she's going to be. You could probably do this without her. The vase has an effect on many people as you continue your journey. An hour after you left the shop, approached over and over, the attention you've received has made you feel special. As you tell person after person about the maker, you wonder if he will have enough vases to go round. You wonder if Grace would be better with one of the new people. You don't seem to have much need of her. She's still just there, in the background.

You head off to find a place to sleep for the night. It's getting dark and the vase looks even more sparkling in the moonlight. You notice eyes watching you and you start to feel nervous. You wonder what to do — you don't know this part of town. The eyes are following you, and footsteps join them. You open your mouth to shout something, but feel Grace's finger on your lips. As you turn towards her, you can't see the vase any more. She has thrown her coat over it, hiding it from prying eyes. The eyes cross by on the other side of the road — they see nothing of value to take, no one to start a fight with, they keep moving. Grace leads the way now. To a small hotel where you stay for the night. The coat covering the vase slips a little as you make your way past the other guests. Where Grace notices a keen interest in the vase, she lets the coat fall further and waits for you to speak to the people who come to ask about it. When she senses interest that could lead to harm, she covers it again, and you move along.

Once in the room, you lie on the bed and find yourself falling asleep before you can help yourself. Your mind is filled with the beauty of the vase, and in dreams it is even more amazing than you remember. You're woken at some point by noisy revellers passing the window. As you jump up, you see Grace, wide awake, sitting next to the vase, polishing it. You're not sure but you think you saw the image of the maker in one of the facets as she turned it. Or maybe it was just a reflection, their family resemblance. You want to speak, to ask her, but sleep overtakes you again.

In the morning, you awake and the sunlight catches the vase. It is more beautiful than yesterday. You are so glad you made the deal with the maker. There's nothing you want more than this. You stare at it until you lose track of time. You can't see Grace, but as your eyes become accustomed to the light you realise she has been there all along. Watching you appreciating the beauty of the vase, and smiling.

So you gather your belongings together and head out. You've left a couple of things in the hotel – books, heavy things that you don't feel like carrying any more – you want to make sure you are showing off the vase as well as you can. You want the maker to get the credit. You continue your travels for several weeks. You go to new places, meet new people; the vase seems to lead you into all kinds of adventures. People want to know about it. You get invited places. Asked deep and interesting questions. You're a lot more interesting since you got it, you think. Life wasn't this much fun before. But eventually it starts to feel heavy. One night, invited to a party by some people who had stopped you in a bar to ask about the vase, you ask Grace to stay at home with it. You don't feel like carrying it all night, and it wouldn't hurt if people wanted to talk about something other than it for a change. So you dress up and head out.

And within an hour or so you're back. Without the vase people weren't so interested, or so interesting. It all just seemed to blend together, but there was no sparkle. Had an OK time, but nothing special. Going out without the vase wasn't as you'd remembered it.

The next night, another party. This time the vase is going too. You don't want another experience like last night. You get caught up in the atmosphere, and at some point you end up passing the vase to Grace, who sits quietly in the corner, polishing it. It's funny, but when she holds it, people don't even seem to notice it's there. Anyway, it frees you up to dance and talk, and whenever anyone asks about the vase, Grace is already at your shoulder, passing it back so you can tell the story. They admire it, ask questions, and get on with the party. With Grace, you are ready for anything.

As time goes on you realise how much a part of your life the vase has become. You love it more than when you first saw it. Every time you look at it you notice a new feature, a different way the light catches it, how its shape seems to alter and yet stay the same. It almost feels part of you. You don't regret the deal for a minute. And Grace has made sure you've never been alone. There has never been a moment when she hasn't helped you, showed you new beauty in the vase or found you a way out of a tricky situation. You don't know how you managed without her. You suspect that she never sleeps.

When you visit old friends, they can see how much you love it. A couple of them have expressed an interest in getting one for themselves – they just want to see how you get on with it first. It looks heavy, and sometimes awkward to carry. You explain about Grace. How she has made all the difference.

Your family can't see its appeal so much – they're relieved you're coming around to visit. After that tour you did, showing off the vase to anyone who wanted to see it, they're just glad you're settling back into normality a bit. They like Grace though. Like the way she is on hand to smooth things over. How when she points out things about the vase, they notice beauty they hadn't seen before. How she puts a hand on your shoulder to remind you to take care of the vase rather than get pulled into an old family tension. How she takes the vase from you so you can help make dinner and wash up. How she doesn't let this commitment you've made become a reason to be less of a real person to those who love and need you. In fact, with her help, you're more of one. By holding it for you, she can do that.

Life is so different. How much can change in a few months! And through all this, Grace is there. Just like her dad said, she cares for the vase, carries it, protects it, and always makes sure you have it to hand. She is always doing things for you, making sure that having the vase is as easy as it can be. When you're tired she helps you to carry it. A couple of times, when you've been distracted, exhausted or even angry and the vase has slipped out of your hands, she's caught it. Sometimes when people have wanted to smash the vase, she has stood in the way and taken the blows. Once, when you'd had a bad day and wanted to smash it, you saw a tear in her eye and you remembered how precious it was. When you've been at work, and you can't remember what on earth possessed you to carry a vase around, she quietly polishes it, and shows you another facet. She calms you, and through that you calm others. When the vase sits on your desk people come and ask about it, just like the maker hoped they would.

And Grace doesn't ask for anything from you. She has been there every time you've needed her, when you haven't even realised it. Then you realise that a year has almost passed. That Grace's obligation is almost up. You wonder if you could do it without her. You leave her at home one day, just to see. Take the vase on the bus, into town, to work, to a restaurant, to a friend's house. Was it always this heavy? This fragile? Did it always get dirty so easily? You still loved it, but would it matter if you left it in the cloakroom for an hour or two? Its value wasn't so obvious when it wasn't being cared for. And you had already talked about it a lot. You had noticed a new colour in the crystal this morning, but did everyone really need to know? They had problems, they didn't want to hear about a vase all the time. Just because looking at it had made your life better, didn't mean it would do anything for them. You snap at people who get in your way, who don't realise what you're carrying. You should call your family, but also you should polish the vase – it really is looking neglected – so which is more important? Surely when Grace was around there was time for both? By the time you get home, you've made a decision. When Grace goes back, the vase goes with her. Without her the vase is the biggest responsibility, the heaviest possession, the most cumbersome and awkward thing you've ever known. You've stopped appreciating its beauty. You don't care if anyone hears about the deal with the maker again. In fact, you'd probably tell them not to go anywhere near the vase unless the maker promised you Grace would be there all day, every day. It was too much to cope with.

So that was that. Decision made. You go to find Grace. She is with the vase, polishing it, smiling broadly. In fact, you've never seen her smile so much. Next to her is a letter. As she is so busy with the vase, you go over and pick it up. You have to know what has made her so happy. You read on:

Dearest, precious Grace,

Thank you so much for doing what I asked of you this year. Even as the maker of the vases that mean so much to both of us, I am still lost for words when I come to describe your beauty. In the past, so many of our precious vases have been smashed, neglected, lost, thrown away or just forgotten about. The decisions people had made to look after and carry our vases have simply been too hard for them. Despite being captivated by the vase, they didn't have the strength to see it through. I didn't want that to happen again.

Deciding to send you out with this vase has changed everything. Somehow I knew your humility, your peacefulness, your concern and your love would be the only thing that could keep the recipient of this vase true to their word. Why did I ever think that handing such a precious thing over without providing your understanding and care would have the same result?!

It is because of you that this vase is still showing its true beauty, and because of you that this vase is still treated as the wonderful gift it is. More and more people are coming to ask for their own vases, just because they have seen the one you have devoted yourself to caring for.

I cannot describe the emotions I felt when I received your letter asking to stay out there and continue to take care of the vase. I know how much it means to you, and how you long for everyone to continue to see its true beauty. While desperately missing you here, I understand the desire behind your request and for the sake of our beautiful creations I will grant you what you ask.

I have now decided that every vase I give out will come with a Grace to care for it. Don't ask me how I'm going to do that – I still have some things to work out!

I don't know when we will see each other again, lovely Grace. Perhaps, as it is time for a new deal to be struck, I can impose my wish once again?

That you will stay with the vase until such time, many years from now, as I call you back to me – you, the vase and our friend to whom I entrusted it. And then you will all come back to me here. Why? So that I will be able to see once again the precious thing I gave away: the vase, which will have become so much more refined from your polishing. And that I will hear from our friend all that they have experienced through keeping the vase, how holding onto that gift changed them, how people responded when they saw it, how much they love it. And we will laugh and dance with joy to be together again, and our friend will realise that in keeping the vase all this time, though only possible because of you, will bring them greater rewards and deeper joy than they can possibly imagine at this minute.

So, my darling Grace, with a heart that is heavy and yet dancing, I bid you farewell, and will wait for that moment when we are together again.

Remember who you are and never tire of expressing that – as if you could!

As I have said to you, since the day you were born, my Grace, my precious, loving Grace, is all conquering and fully, within herself, enough.

All my love

Dad.

Does that do it? Come anywhere near close enough to describing grace? That with the gift of himself that God has given us, he has also given the one thing that could enable us to cope with it.

If you ever take time out to find out what's lurking between the covers of the Bible, you may notice how much of nature God mentions. There is a lot of it – pretty much everything in existence, funnily enough. Lilies, sparrows, lions, falcons, coral, quartz, topaz, rubies, snow, hail, grass, dew, ice, frost, hawks, eagles, an ostrich, even a weird sea creature, to name but a few. And why are they there? Because God wants us to know that he has it covered. There's nothing out there that can surprise him. He knows the weather we're going to face each day, the needs we're going to have, the people we're going to meet. All of it.

And he knows what a monumental strain it's going to be.

He didn't intend for us to do it alone. He gave us grace. He knows we're going to make small steps, some in the right direction, some not. Even with great intentions we can still find ourselves on the wrong path or causing offences we never even imagined. His grace is abounding and overwhelming, like a massive wave that could knock us off our feet but instead covers us without us knowing, and changes everything we allow it to change.

This isn't necessarily about the huge, sweeping stories of personal victory and transformation that great hymns are written about. Just small, everyday steps, moving forward. Putting one foot in front of the other. Tiny little victories barely visible to the naked eye. But not to God's eye. The eye that knows every hair on our heads, every grain of wheat, every sparrow – nothing is lost on him. He wants our lives to succeed. Not by the definition of success that says we have made it if we have everything, but by the definitions he has created so that we could be actually, genuinely joyful no matter what is happening to us. He created grace so that would be an actual possibility.

And what about the times we step back? Slip back. When we thought we knew the ground better than we did, but we still slipped. When we were lonely, tired, angry, wanting things to be different. What about when we wilfully mess up? What about when it just seems too much?

All that glitters

April had made what she calls bad decisions. After several years of marriage, she had ended up involved with another man, and not for the first time. The pain this had caused her husband Robbie and the turmoil she found herself going through as she tried to work out how to get her life back on track, were tearing her apart. She didn't know what to do. Marriage hadn't been all that she'd hoped; unable to have children together, she had found herself adrift and unsure how to move on. In the emptiness she had found herself open to predatory men who offered something that distracted from invasive fertility treatment, disappointment and the uncertain years looming ahead. And now she found herself torn. Swept up in heady romance offered by a man who promised an escape from unhappy times, who could provide everything she could want materially and who claimed to be madly in love with her, she was tempted to leave everything behind and go with him. Concerned family and friends weren't so sure. They could see that April and this man had little in common and the more they learned about his previous relationships and his expectations of this one, the more their concern grew. Robbie tried his best to offer ways to make the marriage work again, putting aside his own hurt to try and re-ignite their romance. April was surprised to see this side of the man she loved after so long. She didn't know what to do. Should she return to the husband who loved her and try to make her marriage work? Or should she seize the opportunity to start again and shut out all that she had lost? Despite everything, she would say she was a Christian, and was trying to be close to God, and to hear him. In her heart she knew that going with the man who encouraged her to leave her marriage behind wasn't the right thing, but she was horribly torn. Finally, she made a decision. A decision not to leave. She didn't know what else she was going to do, but she steeled herself to reject the man she felt madly in love with, and to stay away from the rendezvous he had requested so he would know once and for all that she had chosen him over Robbie.

Her life was in turmoil. Robbie had moved out, to clear his head and put some distance between them. April was living alone for the first time ever, their house for sale, feeling like nothing was certain any more. Her heart desperately wanted to chase after the man who showered her with gifts and wanted to take her away from it all. Her head, and those around her, told her not to go. On the night she was meant to go to him and symbolically show her intention to permanently leave Robbie, she instead stayed at home and watched Sex and the City.

Sex and the City? Really? After all she had gone through, and put Robbie through, this was what she chose to do? Not beg his forgiveness? Not sit in the dark and cry? (She had done a lot of that already.) Not read her Bible, pray and repent? No, none of those things. And I think God was OK with that. Why? Because she had made one small decision in the right direction.

God is bigger than we think. His grace is bigger than we can imagine. I wouldn't be the first person to mention that every small decision we make towards God counts. Would it have seemed more fitting if April had done something more definite and dramatic? If she had gone through a repentance of biblical proportions, noted approvingly by those around her? Maybe. But she did what she could. At that time, when it seemed hardest to do, she turned a little towards God. And I think he was there to welcome her. Encouraging her to step further. Drawing her.

One way or another

Maybe one of the problems that we Christians have created for ourselves is the notion that there is only one way. I don't mean the one way Jesus described himself as: I mean one very particular way of living designed to get to him. Can anyone honestly say they've never met a Christian that they couldn't relate to in the slightest (the opposite in attitudes, dress sense, everything) who was just as convinced as they were that their chosen way of life was perfect? Would it just be too overwhelming if we faced up to the size of the problem, the sheer mass of humanity out there who, to a man (and woman), believe they know best?

For some the response is large-scale meetings and crusades – reach as many thousands and millions as possible in one go with a simple, hopefully life-changing, message. Effective in many parts of the world, apparently, but if that was all that was needed most of us could sit back with a clear conscience while the anointed few got on with it. Those who feel their life's purpose is to preach (who are not – I repeat, NOT – just people who like the sound of their own voice. No, sir) will be pretty sure that this is the most effective way, and as they are the ones we hear most from in church, they will be fairly convincing when telling us that if people aren't hearing it from the front, they're not really hearing it. Get them through the doors and let them hear it as it is. That, they insist, is the way it should be done.

But day to day, where we can't keep people at arm's length and preach at them (not unless we expect them to use the distance as a head start to get as far away as possible), what then? Where church as we know it doesn't seem to be drawing people in? Have you ever thought if only I could get them through the doors one day, and hope they happen to meet people they can identify with (neatly side-stepping the few who might have the opposite effect) and the message is one they can relate to, and no one does anything weird or off-putting, then it will all fall into place? The responsibility is no longer mine.

One-hit blunder

I've been guilty of it myself. When Ella decided to attend an Alpha course, designed for people to discuss the meaning of life, I went along with her on the first night (to make sure she didn't do a runner. And to translate the Christianese if necessary). After that she was on her own – my part was done. Great. I could just sit back and wait for the path of enlightenment to unfold. But it didn't. Instead people, these very helpful Christians, kept jumping in the way. Trying their best to assist, but not really answering her questions in ways she could understand, or even at all. Not explaining what they were talking about in the kind of language she was used to. Not engaging her in conversations she could relate to. As her frustration grew, she wanted to know what she should do. What did they mean when they talked about faith? Were they really expecting people to commit to something they weren't explaining in ways that could be easily understood? What about the questions they wouldn't answer?

I nodded a lot as I listened to her. And that was about it. Tried to figure out the problem so I could let people back at church know where they were going wrong, but still left it almost totally up to them. And the unanswered questions she poured out remained unanswered.

I'm pretty sure God wouldn't have wanted it that way, but I'm afraid that's what I did. Tutted about how "the church" wasn't doing it right, but did nothing as a part of that church to change things.

I just don't believe that's the way it should be. Grace doesn't just live in church. Grace goes with us. Grace is out there, in the everyday mundanity of life and in the worst places on earth. Grace was in the concentration camps in Nazi Germany as people shared their last piece of bread, or even gave their lives so others could live. Grace has been through it all. When we have grace we really do have everything we need. We don't need to wait for the right meetings to take people to; we can just be with them, live alongside them, and grace will make those connections, fill in the gaps and mend the rips.

No really, I'm fine

So often it's the little things we do that make the difference. Nod to an acquaintance in church on Sunday and ask how they are and you will probably not find out much more than "God is good" (Christian shorthand for "Fine, thanks", "I've been better", or "I've lost everything and am about to flee to Azerbaijan to start a new life under an assumed name". Sense the tone. You'll work out which it is). Go out for a drink and spend a couple of hours talking about life and you will probably find out if they really think God is good, and maybe through that conversation they will come closer to knowing it might actually be true because someone listened and cared about what was happening. They could be a small step closer by the end of it, rather than on the verge of running many steps in the opposite direction. Even to Azerbaijan.

If we could learn to relax, things would get a whole lot easier. Grace means we don't have to fix it all. We don't have to have all the answers. We don't have to be the face of disapproval and judgement so that we frighten people into behaving. We don't have to be a one-person support system, anticipating someone's every trauma and spiritual shortcoming. We can just listen and encourage and empathise and love and support. It can take time and be messy. When we can see the mistakes people are making, when they hurt themselves and others, when it interferes with the way we think things should be, it can be hard not to intervene. There may be a time when people need to really face themselves and make some changes, but God isn't necessarily asking us to be the agent of change. He hasn't placed a pressure on us to be his judge, jury and executioner. We can let him work, and we can do our part, whatever that is.

Relax. Don't do it

Let's just not assume that we have to represent all facets of God in every conversation we have. That if someone is having a bad day we must give them a list of helpful verses to memorise and chant in front of the mirror. Or if someone has lost their job, we tell them God has it all in hand, without listening to how they feel, what effects unemployment might be having, what practical help they might need. Alessandro cringed as he recalled a conversation he'd had at church with someone going through a lot of upheaval over relocating overseas. As the person had poured out their heart and frustrations, Alessandro had nodded and said in comforting tones, "It's the same God here as it is there", and given them his best beatific smile. "What a crass thing to say!" he berated himself later. "I must have made them feel awful. Absolutely no help whatsoever."

It's being there for people that really allows grace to flourish. Saying the right thing so we feel that we've represented God well, possibly doesn't represent him at all. Melissa had high standards that were based on her understanding of God and the Bible. She knew what it took to make a good Christian, and when people around her didn't quite make it, she let them know. She didn't mean to be harsh or inflexible, but a time came when some people hesitated to come to her to talk about their lives. Conversations stayed superficial. While people didn't want to fall out with her, they also didn't want to give her access into the inner parts of their lives. They knew when they weren't doing a great job in some areas; what they didn't need was someone telling them so all the time. Especially someone who didn't seem to know what it was like to ever slip up.

Melissa held herself in, lived a quiet and reserved life. Didn't make mistakes. There was no point in trying to explain to her why you'd made a bad decision, or were tempted to do something you shouldn't. She would just tell you not to and wonder why you couldn't have it more together.

But one day Melissa found out that a close friend had gone through a major crisis and she hadn't known anything about it. When it was all over, the person had written, rather than spoken face to face, and explained the situation. They said how in their delicate state they hadn't felt able to face Melissa. That they were telling her now so she'd understand what had happened, but they were sorry, they hadn't been able to let her in at that difficult time because they knew she wouldn't understand. This seemed to be a wake-up call.

Melissa changed.

She had thought all along that what she was doing was best for everyone. Being a rock in times of trouble. Maintaining standards. Representing God. But had she been doing that? Had people needed more than firm words and a standard to live up to? Didn't they need, over all else, love? And understanding? And grace?

Melissa changed.

Became someone who listened and cared, as she always had, but now, instead of trying to fix every situation she heard about, she let people talk. She worked things through with them rather than telling them what they should do. She allowed herself to understand what it must be like to be in those situations.

And people opened up to her again. Appreciated the advice she gave because it came with empathy and grace.

It's going to be OK

I need to hear that once in a while. I'm sure you do too. To know that no matter how hard a situation is, how much I might have messed up, hope is not lost. That to turn inwards at this point, to lean towards self-loathing or anger isn't going to help. One of the best pieces of advice I've ever been given is also one of the simplest, and almost every day at some point it crosses my mind. It is simply this: be kind to yourself. Why do I think of it so often? Because every day there are so many opportunities to do the exact opposite. Ever heard someone usually mild mannered shout, "You are such an IDIOT" (or something much worse) and then realised they're talking to themselves? We all do it. Treat ourselves much more harshly than we do others. OK, I'm sure you can think of a few people who've definitely treated you a lot more harshly than that and probably never have a bad word to say about themselves, but you take my point. We can be our own worst enemy, our own harshest critic, the meanest bully we've ever met.

Watch out for it tomorrow when you close that document without saving it, or have a cigarette when you'd sworn you'd given up for good, or lose your keys when you're already running late, or drop red wine on the cream carpet. Do you respond as you would if a friend did it? Or do you let rip with some major aggression, aimed squarely at yourself? A lot of us are in the habit of judging ourselves severely. Beating ourselves up over every slip-up and mistake.

We owe it to ourselves to find a better way through these things, so that we don't get stuck repeating our mistakes. It's what God wants for us too. Not to condemn us or label us, but to free us from them. So we don't need to carry the burden.

Seconds out. Round 2...

Too often we think that once we've crossed the line into the unknown territory of the Christian world it only takes one mess-up before we're out on our ear. Perhaps it doesn't take much to see us out of favour for good. At one church I attended we used to think up ways to "go out with a bang". If you're going to get kicked out of church, make sure it's memorable. Rugby-tackle the speaker. Come in a gorilla suit and heckle throughout in a foreign accent. Turn all the chairs to face the back. Streak. The list was endless (we possibly weren't concentrating fully on the wonderful meetings at the time).

But none of those things actually made a difference to grace, or to how much God loved us (though we may possibly have needed to find a new church if we'd carried them out. I'll let you know how the experiments progress).

But that's not how grace works. Slipping up isn't the end of the world. It really isn't. You probably won't find any Christian who'll tell you to carry on as you were and no one will mind – and I think that's for the best – but this is about what happens if you do make a mistake, even a wilful one. Let's assume you're generally not living as though you don't care. That you're not trying to see what you can get away with, test some invisible boundaries, act out a teenage rebellion again. Let's assume that you know God loves you. That you're trying to figure out what that means, and what life could look like from now on. This is about putting one foot in front of the other, in the right direction and wanting to continue that way, then just not despairing if it doesn't go right first time. Or even second. Or even tenth. No, really. There isn't a magic number after which you've run out of chances. I'm not saying God likes it when we go back to things we should know better than to revisit, I'm just saying he doesn't want to turn his back for good. Grace keeps him looking in our direction. He loves us passionately. He doesn't want anything to come between us and him. He doesn't like it when we go back to things that put barriers in the way, when we turn away from him.

No more sticky situations

But it's good to be making progress, for our own sakes. So we don't have to live feeling defeated. Danny said, when he had struggled with various habits for a number of years, "Each time I slip up I'm so hard on myself. There is no grace. Not from him – there's loads from him. I just don't have any for myself." He had grown tired of carrying the weight of things he didn't want or need any longer and he'd had enough. "I just don't want to keep juggling it all any more. It's exhausting. I want to be free of all that 'stuff'. Just move on once and for all." And I guess that's the point. For our own sakes, freedom. We don't need to be bound. It's a waste of energy. It's what God wants for us too. Not to be torn constantly between what he has planned for us and what we find irresistible even though it harms us. Does that mean that God is waiting for us to step out of line then? And what happens when we do?

During my stint in the corporate world, I jetted off to a large international gathering designed to educate, entertain and stimulate the workforce into bigger and better sales. I was there more as an observer than a participant and, as events unfolded, found myself very relieved this was the case. The company had a friendly image but very high expectations. Everyone had to pull their weight, no excuses. Senior executives, god-like figures worshipped by all, were always watching. In order to put their money where their mouths were, they would personally support individual products, encouraging staff to rev up their efforts in making great sales of these particular commodities. Personal pride and executive egos were invested in the subsequent performance of these precious items.

As thousands gathered in the auditorium, ready to celebrate great results, onto the stage strode one extremely important man. He had spent the year putting his reputation and energies into one extremely important product. Along with helping to run the company, that is. None of the thousands of employees in the room that day could fail to know what he cared about more than anything else at that moment. Velcro. Yep, he'd put his money on Velcro. Anticipation rippled around the room as he opened his mouth to announce who had sold the most of the helpfully sticky item within the last twelve months. A name was spoken. A man somewhere in the dimly lit back rows was ushered to his feet, ready to receive plaudits and congratulations. There was just one tiny problem. He hadn't sold the most Velcro. In fact, he'd sold the least. In the whole company. And he'd been found out. No shiny award for him that day. Instead he was led onto the stage and behind a curtain. We waited. Were there to be gun shots? Blood-curdling screams? The sound of a trapdoor opening? Silence. And then he appeared again, dressed involuntarily in a white body stocking, covered from head to foot in...no, could it be...Velcro?

At the other side of the stage, a large, round target was wheeled on. Behind the uncertain-looking victim a piece of cannon-like apparatus was moved into place. As he looked from one to the other, the nature of his punishment unfolded. There was no grace here. There was, however, a compulsory opportunity to fly, with thousands of witnesses looking on. Across the stage and slap-bang into a waiting target. He was fired across the stage – watched by hundreds of people silently thanking anyone who'd bought Velcro from their store that year – and landed with no dignity whatsoever, at a strange, awkward angle, where he hung for all to see. Like a fly in a spider's nylon web. The target was wheeled off stage and the razzmatazz resumed. Come to think about it, I didn't see him return to his seat. He may well still be there now.

I have a feeling that may be the way some of us see God. Waiting for us not only to slip up, but just simply not be good enough, so he can step in and splat us. Public humiliation, parading our mistakes, wanting us to be demeaned and diminished so we know who's boss. I don't think he has the spiritual equivalent of a human-sized cannon and target though. He's just not vindictive. That's why he has grace. Not so we can know better and do it anyway.

If you know grace, why would you want to step out of it? If you really, really know grace, you'd never want to go away again.

It doesn't *really* matter, does it?

Maybe we've got used to grace somewhat, or at least the definition we understand. A casual grace that shrugs off our little indiscretions and turns a blind eye to our vices. Have we got to a point of thinking that grace somehow means it doesn't matter what we do? I've heard it said that "God doesn't mind" when we do things we know we really shouldn't. Doesn't he? After all, he knows each one of us so personally that maybe the little things just don't matter at this moment compared to where he knows we're going. He isn't the type, as the old saying goes, to use a sledgehammer to crack a nut.

Craig was a farmer, a rough, outdoorsy guy who didn't consider himself polished or refined. His speech was earthy, to say the least. It was just his regular, everyday language. He realised many Christians didn't swear (not so colourfully anyway), and while it meant nothing to him, he wondered if maybe there was good reason. He didn't know if God minded, but he'd been swearing for so many years he didn't know any other way. So he thought he'd ask. "God, if you want me to stop swearing you'll have to do it."

The next day he was riding along in his tractor, as farmers are prone to do, and he had a sudden realisation. He hadn't sworn. He thought back over every conversation he'd had with the men he worked with, not a single thing that would make the vicar blush. He'd stopped overnight, and with no effort on his part. For the rest of the day, he was surprised to hear himself. The same person but somehow different.

Craig's experience made me think. His swearing was just a habit, the language of his surroundings, no deeper root, no hidden anger waiting to burst out. When he had asked God to stop it if God would rather it wasn't there, it had stopped immediately. But what if that had been a symptom of something deeper? Something that God would rather was dealt with properly and not just airbrushed out of memory.

That's grace too. Sometimes when we keep holding on to old habits it's because they're the symptom of something deep within. Old wounds. Unhealed emotional pain. Inner emptiness. Something that means we need a crutch. Not in the physical sense, but unconsciously we need to rely on something to fill the void, to comfort us, to take away the pain. And, until the right time, grace prevents that thing being ripped away from us, leaving us exposed and vulnerable. I don't want to frighten you, but you may find in time to come that it will happen to you. Little things that just seem to get in the way at the moment will eventually be worked out, in a deeper way, leaving you free. It's nothing to be scared of. Grace will be right there.

A graceful exit

The Bible says to "work out your salvation with fear and trembling". Not exactly light-hearted. Do we really want to go there? Put ourselves through the wringer? Is that what it means: to be constantly checking ourselves for mistakes? I think God just wants us to grasp what it's really all about. Not make excuses for ourselves and the things that hold us back. Not measure ourselves by standards we can't possibly live up to on our own. Not spend our time condemning ourselves for what went before and where we are now. He wants to be right there in the middle of where we are. He already is, whether we know it or not. Grace is there too. Ready to deal kindly with us. Let's not turn away, be happy as we are, not knowing what we could be. Sometimes it's the easiest thing in the world. Like Craig, we'll wake up and it'll be gone. Sometimes it's like ripping off a plaster. Sometimes it will cost us more than we think we can bear. All I can say is that it will be worth it. Grace will cover us completely.

4. Freedom. Like a prisoner who has their own key

In the words of the great poet Georgios Kyriacos Panayiotou, if you're going to do it, do it right (alright, you've sussed it. It's George Michael). The only problem is that one person's right may well be another person's absolutely, definitely wrong (in case you were wondering I'm pretty much always right. Saves a lot of debate to clear that up now). It happens at work, at home, everywhere. Just feel the tension. Out in the big, wide world, it can be far too easy to be influenced by others, sometimes good, sometimes bad. And what about in Christian circles, when the opinions that are floating about can seem a million miles away from what we're used to?

Suzie had a radical new haircut. She was young and gorgeous and would have looked lovely if she'd been attacked by a maniac with a strimmer and a grudge. Everywhere she went that week the compliments flowed. Everyone liked it, and the more they liked it, the more she liked it. She officially rocked. Then, a few days later, she bumped into a colleague. Distracted, the colleague eyed up the hairstyle, mentioned it had been cut well, and...that was all. Suzie panicked. That's it, she said later that evening. Finally someone has been honest. Everyone else was just being polite. It didn't look good and she was stuck with it. What was she going to do now?! If only I'd caught her before she shaved her head... Just kidding. Well... How about do nothing?

The haircut looked the same as it had a week ago. A millimetre or two longer, maybe.

It still suited her.

She still liked it.

Or she had. Now, the truth was out. Everyone secretly hated it and had sneakily communicated their thoughts through the mouth of a distracted woman. Who was to know such things went on? That casually muttered opinion suddenly invalidated the fifty other spontaneous affirmations and sent Suzie into a downward spiral. Even if the passing remark had been considered and she meant it from the bottom of her heart (and don't forget all she said was that it was well cut. She didn't vomit on her shoes and run screaming from the building) it was still only her opinion.

Suzie didn't need the stress of assessing every comment, interpreting every look, detecting subtle disapproval from every quarter. Who does? And what difference did it make anyway? We all have opinions. Our way of seeing the world. And they are always right. (Just kidding. Mine are, so yours can't be. Unless you wholeheartedly agree with me, of course.) Opinions are the filter through which all our decisions are made; in some ways they are the most important thing about us. They affect what we do, what we don't do and how we view the lives of those around us.

Everything we do is shaped by opinion, either our own or someone else's.

It becomes an issue when our opinions become the only standard by which we judge life. We can end up unhappy with everyone and everything around us unless they conform to our opinion of what they should be – and who's to say we're right anyway? Or we can be equally unhappy if we depend on the opinions of others to tell us how we should be. Anyone fancy a healthy balance instead? There is a certain liberation in putting other people's opinions in their rightful place.

All's fair in love and church

It can be especially tough to do that in church or around our Christian chums, when opinions can arrive in the guise of unimpeachable spiritual truth. Over the years, I've found that while there are some things we should agree on so that we are all going in roughly the same direction, there are plenty of others that are just personal choice or interpretation.

It becomes a problem only when people become convinced that it's more than that. That they have the inside scoop on whether we should kneel down to pray or not (yes, it matters deeply to some people) or whether women should get to wear the poshest dresses in church or just the men (I'm only talking about vicars, don't panic).

It's pretty easy to be intimidated by an opinionated person, especially when they may seem to have their lives much more together than us (on the surface at least), and it takes work to separate good advice from just opinion. It would be foolish to isolate ourselves from people who can help us through the difficult times in life just because we think we know best. Wisdom that comes our way is a valuable thing, no matter how it comes or who it comes from, and sometimes that can mean surprising sources. But how do we learn to differentiate between the two? Jennifer used to end every argument or debate with the crowning phrase "I'm entitled to my opinion!" cancelling out all objections.

I wonder about this. Are we really entitled to our opinions? As a Christian, I think I'm more entitled to God's opinion than mine. When I look at someone, does it matter what I think about them, or is it infinitely more important what he thinks? And the fact is, I already know what he thinks. He loves them so much that he did everything he did just to know them. He thinks they are amazing, unique, beautiful and precious beyond words. He has all the time in the world for them. He knows everything they've ever done and he loves them as much as he ever did. What does it matter what I think compared to that? That they have a weird laugh or strange hair or unusual personal habits? Don't I have a duty to see beyond my prejudices and reactions to take on his opinion, as quickly as possible?

Yes, they may be difficult, and while God may not be asking us to be their best friends, he is still asking us to do what we can and try to see them his way. Not to focus on the issues. Not to be in conflict.

The Bible calls it living in peace with everyone, as far as we can. We don't have to fix them; we don't have to avoid having healthy boundaries; we just have to remember we have grace right there with us, helping to make it work.

After all, how do we know they're not struggling to see us in a positive light? (Hard to believe, but don't rule it out.) The benefit of the doubt can go a long way in helping to build relationships, even casual or superficial ones.

If only she'd listen to me...

The same goes for the myriad of situations we face every day, our own and those around us. What our friends and family are doing, or what we think they should be. Work. Politics, current affairs, money and celebrity. Is it really any of my business? Wars have started over opinions. Is there any need for me to join the throng of voices over a celebrity scandal, troubled marriage, mysterious super injunction or disagreement at church, with a knowing shrug and "well, if you ask me..." as if that will change anything for the better? Adding to the general noise and hot air. Can I really be bothered? Would I want that kind of speculation if I was in a situation people wondered about? Often enough, our opinions are based on a distortion. We can't possibly know the inside out of even a tiny percentage of the things we spout forth about so eloquently. We see, we think we know and we must share what springs to mind. But we don't really know. Even our closest friends are something of a mystery to us. We don't know what they're thinking in the deepest recesses of their minds. We don't really know what happens in their relationships. How can we know the intricacies of anyone else's situations and feel qualified to comment? And how easily can we be drawn into unhelpful gossip?

Controlling? No, I just have high standards for you

Here comes the issue. What if our opinions become so important to us that we override the wishes of others to ensure our opinions set the tone? Or we react badly when they are ignored? Or become determined to inflict them on others and respond with criticism, withdrawal or some other punishment when this doesn't happen?

This is control. Control ain't good.

Judy realised her other half was controlling when she woke up with a horrified start in the early hours of the morning, thinking she was having a vivid nightmare about wrestling. Instead of being head-locked by The Rock (which, strangely, is the fantasy of one girl I know), she found she was being physically manhandled into an entirely new sleeping position by the concerned Mr Judy.

"What are you doing?" she asked, drowsy but wondering why her legs were being straightened under the duvet. "You'll be more comfortable like this," other half told her, "you'd never have slept for long lying like you were before."

Unable to sleep, he had assessed her blissful state, decided it was inadequate and felt compelled to intervene. Having finally manoeuvred her limbs into his chosen arrangement and explained his actions, he dropped off, satisfied that all was well in his world. The newly wrestled Judy? She spent the rest of the night wide awake, partly stunned, largely furious and definitely not more comfortable.

There is a natural conclusion to the desire to control, and that is to see everything around us fall in with our own opinions, even if that means rearranging people while they sleep.

From telling people how to dress, to how to have their hair, to what job they should take, or leave, to whom they should marry or where they should live, we might have it all covered.

And then what?

Where will it all end up?

What if I had very clear ideas about what's right for you? And of course, I only want the best for you. I have your best interests at heart. How could you ever doubt that? Let's assume you comply, take on board everything I say to you…

Number one fan

I wish you lived closer, I feel like I hardly ever see you. It would be great. We could see each other at weekends and in the evenings. And you'd probably save money too, in the long run. This isn't such a nice area, but I think you'd be happier.

Yes, you think, it would be nice to see more of each other. And you've spent a lot of time on your flat, making it home, but nowhere is forever. It would mean a longer commute, but what's that compared to quality time with friends? You move closer.

I worry about how much you work. You always seem to be at that place. I don't think they really appreciate you. I just don't want to see you taken advantage of. You're worth so much more. And it's not like it's that close any more, not since you moved. You could look for something round here instead, couldn't you?

Hmm, good point, you think. I have been putting in the hours, and for what? You decide to resign, and despite your boss telling you that you're doing really well and promotion is just round the corner, you leave. He would say that. It's time to go somewhere where you'll get noticed. In the meantime, you'll scrape by. Things will be fine. At least you aren't so stressed. And you've got friends who care.

I hope you don't mind me saying this, but... I'm not sure he really loves you. You don't seem as happy as you used to. He doesn't seem to be around so much these days – I mean, do you know where he is? Doesn't he like your new place? Just because it's smaller and further away from his? Are you sure he's right for you? I just want what's best for you. Someone who really appreciates how great you are. Not for you to have to settle for anything less. Yes, you think, good point. He hasn't made much of an effort lately. Has he? I suddenly don't really feel appreciated. Never mind how much fun he is to be with, and how he looked after me when I was sick last week, and that lovely holiday last year. I don't want to settle for less than I deserve. And that dinner he made last night was too little, too late. Yes, you think, I'd be better off on my own for a while. Spend time with friends who really care about me.

I'm worried you're not eating properly. You seem to be getting very skinny. You really aren't taking care of yourself, are you? You need a bit of looking after. Get you back to your former glory. It'll be great. Then you can borrow that top of mine you said you liked – it's hanging off you at the moment. Not a good look.

Oh, you think, am I looking that bad? Well, she would only say it out of concern. And that cake she made, what a nice gesture, when she's been on that diet for so long. Nice of her to bother when she's got so many other things to think about. You tuck in.

I've been meaning to speak to you about your car. I know money's a bit tight since you left work and haven't found anything else (you did the right thing. I'm sure your perfect job is just around the corner) but now you're in a flat without proper parking, and you don't need it to see *him* any more, why don't you save the money? Get rid of it. Get a bike! We could go cycling together. It'd be fun!

Yeah, you think. That makes sense. I could do with saving some money, now that I'm not working, and this flat, well it's costing a lot more than expected, what with the plumbing problem and the boiler breaking. And a bike would be a healthier option. So you sell your car.

You know that holiday you mentioned? The one with those girls you used to work with. The loud ones who always seemed hung-over when we bumped into them? Well, I was thinking. I mean, now we've both got bikes, why don't we go on a cycling holiday instead? Much cheaper, and I'm sure it would be much more fun than watching them get drunk every night.

I guess so, you think. I haven't seen much of them lately, now I'm so far away, and don't have a car and don't see them at work any more. Don't really go out either, especially now I can't fit into my going-out clothes, after eating all that cake. So, you decide, I suppose I'll tell them I can't make it. May as well go cycling instead. I'm not sure about your new haircut. I mean, it probably looked great in the magazine, but, well, not everyone has the cheekbones, do they? A rounder face suits quite a different look...

Oh dear, you think, is it true? Has no one else been honest enough to tell me? Not that I've really seen anyone else lately. Maybe that's why? No one wants to be seen with someone with hair Elton John would get a refund on. I'm going to buy a hat until it grows out.

I know it's probably only a temporary measure, and I don't want to sound rude, but as your friend I just want the best for you, so don't be offended. But that hat...

See where I'm going with this?

Scared yet?

Get into a cycle of control and you may find the brakes are missing. People who love us generally want the best for us. That's a good thing. If that love is distorted, it's not good. For us or anyone else. We can't fill someone else's emptiness or take away their frustration by letting ourselves be manipulated into being what they want. We can't take away their fear of the unknown by allowing our lives to be rigidly managed. If we're going to act on someone's recommendations, we just need to make sure our definitions match. And if not, be confident to go our own way. Not feel that what they want is something we should take on just to avoid offence. Not unless we want to end up homeless, jobless, loveless, friendless, car-less, over-eating and wearing unflattering hats.

Does it always have to be about boys?

There have been various times when I've had boyfriends who haven't met with the approval of some of my friends. Not because they've been mean or violent or anything sinister, just because something hasn't clicked – and because they had other ideas about what I should be doing. On one occasion a housemate asked me to end a relationship because my paramour had an accent that reminded her of someone she went to school with. She made things difficult whenever he came around, loudly announcing she was going out and pointedly slamming doors and generally being less than pleasant. In the times between his visits she would continually remind me of how much his voice grated on her. She really didn't want him around, and she didn't stop going on about it until he was sent packing. I can't have liked him that much, but even so.

On another occasion, one of my friends objected to a gentleman caller on the basis that having him around would mean less opportunity for us to go out and do our own thing. She had rarely been single since her mid-teens and had recently found herself unexpectedly alone. She wanted to live it up. She didn't want her partner in crime tied up in a previous arrest. So she tried to persuade me that I'd be better off without him. That we didn't need him hanging about. There were better out there. I can't have been that attached, as I eventually kissed him goodbye. Shortly after my friend coupled up again, and funnily enough wasn't too worried how I spent my time any more.

You may be wondering by now if I have a handle on one side and come in useful when people want a cup of tea. Fear not, I'm not a complete mug. I'm not averse to giving or receiving advice that helps anyone make good decisions for fear of appearing controlling. Often those who know us well know exactly what to say, and do so because they care. One friend, listening to my tales of romantic woe over several months, would counter each tale with a knowing nod and the comment "My ex used to do that". The picture of her ex built in my mind until one day I responded, "Your ex wasn't a nice guy, was he?" She looked me in the eyes and said clearly and slowly, "NO." It took a long time for my clouded head to realise that all the things that had made her relationship unworkable were all the things present in mine. I can be a little slow sometimes. Rather than nag me, criticise him, roll her eyes and get exasperated, she listened, supported and helped me to reach the conclusion that was right for me. To be out of the relationship. There was nothing in it for her (except a bit less earache). She was just looking out for me.

But it's only because I care...

What we need to watch out for is advice or support that seems to benefit the people giving it more than it benefits us. Lydia had met a man at church who seemed nice. She was going through a lot at the time, and he always seemed to be around to offer practical and emotional support. She didn't know many people in the church, or the area, so they ended up meeting up for dinner, chatting and texting often, and he always seemed to say the right thing, never tired of asking about her problems, in fact, didn't really want to talk about much else.

One evening, as he drove her home from a night out she remarked that things had been tough lately. Straight away he said, "It's OK, everything will be fine. You've got me now." She wondered what this meant, but not for long. Conversations started to focus more and more on what she was doing wrong, how much help she needed from him, how fortunate it was that he was there to make things right. They weren't romantically involved, but things seemed to intensify. It wasn't until her situation started to improve that things took a negative turn.

One day, excited about a development at work, she told him, expecting him to be as pleased as she was. Instead he acted as though she hadn't spoken. She didn't push the matter and was surprised several hours later when he snapped, "Right, what's going on with this work thing?" and demanded the full story. She explained, and then at the end of the story asked why he hadn't responded when she first mentioned it.

He exploded. Shouting about her ego, about her need to outdo him and more. She was stunned. There had been no warning of this before now. He had always been competitive but this was something new. She walked away, leaving him to cool down. That night he apologised but couldn't explain himself. Things weren't the same again. She distanced herself, not wanting to provoke more outbursts.

A few months later, another issue arose in her life. Within hours of hearing about it, he was there again, offering support, doing what he could to make things better, letting her know how much he could do for her.

But when things improved, he backed off. Wouldn't respond to invitations to regular social events. He only wanted to be there when she was down, telling her how he could make it all right for her if only she'd let him.

When things were fine, he couldn't deal with it: his chance to feel in control was gone.

Lydia is relieved she realised when she did. When she sees him around now, he won't even make eye contact.

You know where you can stick your bow

It takes a bit of wisdom to recognise when we are being controlled and when we're not. My dear old dad was an expert in all things packaging related. Boxes, presents, cases, anything: if it involved folding paper and fitting things together he was there. The Picasso of the packing case. Which meant that he always knew best. If I was hurriedly wrapping a gift before rushing out to a birthday party, I would sense hawk-like scrutiny from the corner of the room. With every fold, he would strain his neck to check optimum angles were being maintained. When the sticky tape was unfurled there would be a sharp intake of breath if edges weren't aligned.

Let's not even mention the painstaking application of gift bows. Shudder.

One day it was all too much. He was concentrating on the process more than I was, staring like an obsessed scientist, and after his third top tip for wrapping the perfect present, I snapped. "You are such a control freak!" I screamed at him. He looked shocked. "I was only trying to help," he said, unsure what he'd done wrong. I was in no mood to back down. Grabbing my half-wrapped gift I stormed out of the room.

The party wasn't that much fun. I didn't feel great about my outburst. When I spoke to my mum later, she said quietly, "I really don't think your dad is a control freak. He just always wants to help. Especially where gift-wrapping is concerned." I knew she was right. There was nothing motivating him other than the desire to see the parcel look as good as it could, because that was how he ticked (who knew anyone could care so much about gift wrap?). He couldn't help but notice. He didn't want to put me down, or have things his own way, or exert his authority. He wasn't that kind of man. I can genuinely say I've never met a kinder, more helpful or more generous man. He had no ulterior motive. I had reacted wrongly, perceived an attempt to control that wasn't there.

All I need now is the mini-me

The extreme output of having things our own way is the desire for world domination. I haven't met too many people like that. Well... no, no, I really haven't (you know who you are). But there are many more who shrink their world down to a controllable size and try to manage everything in it. What happens then? Unhappiness, generally, and probably a few tension headaches. For the person who wants things their way and doesn't get it, as well as for the people around them. Life is full of unexpected twists and turns. Minimising exposure to them isn't really a long-term solution. It's just not possible to control what happens forever. And the fun, the spontaneity, the unexpected pleasures and joys of life are lost to us. God's not big on control, despite what you may have heard. He's big on surprises though, and putting us in places where we are positioned to receive the best things he has for us. His plans can seem bizarre. Out of step with everyone we know. Moving the opposite way to the direction in which society seems to be heading in. God can be steering us, leading us, to things he has for us. He is not trying to control us.

Controlling people may not even be aware of it. There may just be a creeping expectation that things will be a certain way. They may call it tradition. Or "just the way we do things". Or call it decency and worry what friends, relatives or the neighbours think (shame masquerading as "other people's opinions". The neighbours probably haven't said anything. They may well be too busy worrying about what you think). They may even suffer anxiety or depression when things don't go the way they want.

Controlling people make it difficult for the people around them, who have to adapt. Who become hypersensitive to what will cause upset, silence, withdrawal, disappointment or outbursts of anger. They dread the phone ringing, knowing another lecture or outburst is on the way. Missed call after missed call until the person gets to say their piece. Or days, even weeks, of silence, as a punishing withdrawal is initiated. Or they may not adapt. They may continue to do the things that irritate, inviting angry responses as a way of asserting their own control, or as a silent rebellion. It can all get very messy.

Maybe keep a couple of toys *in* the pram?

Erin describes herself as a spoilt child when she doesn't get her own way (and she can't really get away with being called a girl any more, no matter how much she moisturises). Despite her best efforts to keep life under control, problems came, and her reactions to them escalated. God's on my case, she said. Ah, that frequently used expression. Christian shorthand to describe the times when the habits we tolerate, the problems we've run away from and things in our past that we haven't dealt with, which may be affecting how we behave now, start to rise up in unexpected ways, requiring us to face them. Erin found herself exploding at things that were out of her control, things that had only irritated her before. She knew this wasn't the end of the matter, that she wasn't going to spend the rest of her life enraged. God wanted her to face the reasons behind the outbursts and deal with them, not keep going over the same old ground. For her sake, not his. So she could be free to live without the stress and anger.

Life just isn't that controllable. When we control we may avoid the unexpected nastiness of existence, as much as that can ever happen, but we also avoid the unexpected fun and joy. We also can't be sure that the things we try to avoid won't pop up where we try to prevent them and not quite in the form we imagined. What would make us want to control? Fear of what might happen, or of what might not. Deep-rooted fears that we may not even be conscious of might be at the core of our opinions and our need to control what happens in our lives.

Let's get to the main thrust

I heard about a hen night a few years ago where the bride had laid out a very specific code of conduct with very specific standards of specific behaviour for all involved. Specifically. Events were carefully planned. Top of the list of dos and don'ts was that there was not to be that staple of the modern pre-marriage ladies' outing, the stripper. Under no circumstances was the blushing bride to be ambushed by the oily charms of a fake fireman or muscular cowboy. Dinner was booked at a lively but respectable restaurant in town. Alongside the party was another hen outing, considerably more boisterous, and not holding back on any of the great traditions of prenuptial celebration. As the evening progressed respectably, the polite conversation that rippled around the first table over the pizzas was suddenly drowned out by the throbbing bass of the classic and moving love song "I'm too sexy". The party at the next table began to whoop and cheer. Through the smoky haze and suggestively shaped helium balloons, a figure appeared. Baby oil glinting from every wobbling surface, he gyrated his way across the room. The bride looked horrified. The hens uneasy. Had someone gone against the great decree? There was silence at the table, though not at the table next door. The shrieks of delight rose to a crescendo as the leather-clad lothario introduced himself one by one to the guests at the second party, where he was, it quickly turned out, an invited and very welcome guest.

I use the term "introduced" loosely. There was no shaking of hands. The language of his other body parts said it all. As he danced his way round the table to the squealing second bride, he had worked up quite a sweat. He picked a spot behind her and concentrated his energies, and his, er, specific charms, on the happy lady. There was only one problem. The brides were sitting back to back. Which meant that our friend, Bride A, was directly behind the gentleman visitor and in the full path of his non-conversational side. Polite chitchat on table A faltered as every few seconds the sweaty posterior of the thrusting stud appeared over the bride's shoulder, missing her horrified face by a millimetre. And so it came to pass that the bride who hadn't wanted a stripper at all, got one. And much more of him than she expected.

Not all attempts to avoid our worst fears will come back to haunt us in this way. Hopefully not, anyway – no one wants an irrational fear of leather pouches and baby oil for the rest of their lives. And then there are times that control leads to something much more serious.

Family values

Well-meaning people can find their best intentions backfiring. Nadia had felt controlled all her life. Growing up in a rigidly Christian home, she had been sheltered from the perils of the outside world by strict but concerned parents. Everything was taboo. The world was described as an evil place, full of terrible things. It was a lonely life. Marginalised at school, she felt ugly, boring and freakish. She didn't have friends, wasn't included in anything that went on. Boys didn't notice her. She was a non-person. And this suited family life fine. No temptations, no distractions, nothing to lead her off the straight and narrow. But it was unsustainable. The world wasn't going to stay away indefinitely. As she progressed through her teens, Nadia found her footing a little more. Got a Saturday job, grew into her looks, realised she wasn't going to be ignored forever. She started to wonder about the opportunities that might be waiting out there for her. She met a boy. Not the nice boy her family had hoped for, several years in the future. A completely unsuitable boy, whose values seemed non-existent.

And as sex had been unmentionable except as an evil to avoid, Nadia was unprepared for what might be involved. She hadn't gone away from the Christian values that had been instilled since childhood and, despite the growing relationship, she held on to what she calls her moral stance. This wasn't enough for her family though. Ultimatums were issued. Nadia, suddenly feeling liberation, refused to give him up. Even though she wasn't sleeping with him, and none of her parents' worst fears were being realised, the insistence continued. She wouldn't listen. The ultimatums grew more intense. One day things came to a head. Leave him or leave home. Thinking this was a bluff, and there was no way her parents would ever throw her out – after all, having been kept on such a tight leash, sudden freedom was never going to be offered on a plate – she refused again to give him up. An hour later she was standing at a bus stop with her clothes in bags around her feet. This was no bluff. Her boyfriend, laid back to the point of catatonia, helpfully got himself thrown out of home so they could be together. They found temporary places to stay, bedding down with whoever was kind enough to offer space for a few nights. Nadia was still holding on to her values and her virginity. This wasn't about anything other than a battle for control; she just didn't want to be told what to do. She still had standards she intended to hold on to, no matter what. But they were living in limbo; staying with friends couldn't last forever. Her boyfriend said he'd found them a more permanent place.

It was, literally, everything her family had ever tried to keep her from. A converted church which now housed hard-living drug addicts. The parties were non-stop. Orgies was probably a more accurate description. Nadia shut herself in their dingy room as all she heard around her, twenty-four hours a day, was sex. People going from room to room, not caring who they were with. Other people would arrive, ready to drink, get high and join in. And, despite being surrounded by all of this, she still wasn't in a sexual relationship with her boyfriend. Going home was no longer an option. She was stuck in a half-life which offered nothing good. And then things got much, much worse. Nadia was raped. Not by a stranger, but by one of the men in the house. She felt as if her world had ended. And then she found out she was pregnant. On her eighteenth birthday she miscarried.

She had never felt so alone. Returning at last to the family home, anger and violent outbursts made it impossible for her to stay, and she was soon on the move again. She says now how vulnerable she felt. There is no self-pity as she describes what she went through back then. Now happily married with a family, Nadia looks back at that time in disbelief that she isn't scarred by her experiences. It made me think how dreadfully sad her family must have been when their attempts to protect her had ended in such trauma and heartbreak. We just can't control other people without a backlash, and that could see them rushing headlong into all the things we never wanted to touch them. They won't see what's best for them. They will react against us.

Fig leaves optional

Or it can all turn out very differently. What if we don't react? What if, instead, when we are controlled we start to feel shame and internalise the feelings? I don't think that's God's plan for us either. The church can be good at shame. Christians can get used to it as a constant companion. I had an epiphany once. Driving along, music blaring. The dulcet tones of Oasis informing me that I should feel no shame. I thought for a moment. Feel no shame. No shame at all? None? About anything? Aside from Liam Gallagher, says who? Well, God as it turns out. That was his plan right from the start. For people to live in a paradise he had designed purely as a place where he could spend time with them. They were naked, the Bible says, and felt no shame. No shame? Naked? (Had cellulite been invented then?) When God is popping round for a chat after work? Wow, they must have been confident.

They were, until it all went wrong. Until they fell headlong into the trap. Their eyes were opened, they had knowledge of everything. Of good and evil. And that brought shame. When God dropped by that day, they hid. The Old Testament mentions it a lot. God talks about his enemies being put to shame. He doesn't want it for his children though. That's why when Jesus came and mended the way so we could get back into relationship with God, shame is mentioned specifically. That we don't need it. We won't be put to shame.

So if shame isn't compulsory for us, why do we, who know God loves us, still let it control us? Can we find a way to get things back to the way he intended? Wouldn't you rather spend the rest of your life so confident that God loved you that you didn't need other people's approval? I don't mean become an egotistical nightmare, convinced we never put a foot wrong and no one else puts a foot right, or even sceptical of other people's opinions when they may be just what we need to hear. I'd never want to be without the loving, accountable friendships God has brought into my life. I'm talking instead about having a certainty and affirmation that goes beyond self-confidence. Letting God show you who you are; nothing we come up with could be better than that.

5. Pride comes before a fall. Generally not helped by ridiculously high heels

I've never been cool. Never. Not deep down. Though often accused of swanning – or even elegantly gliding on a good day – too frequently the mirage of sophistication has come crashing down as I, literally, have come crashing down. It's not all about image. It can't be, otherwise I'd have nothing. On a recent social outing I left my heel wedged between two paving stones and carried on regardless. Not quite regardless. I was suddenly a couple of inches taller on one side than the other.

I looked ridiculous. This was no Marilyn Monroe wiggle. But there wasn't much I could do. There was no mobile heel bar conveniently passing by, no kindly cobblers' convention in town, rushing to my aid. I had no option but to lurch onwards. Ignored by the previously close friend, who made sure they were a few steps ahead, deliberately oblivious. Not ignored by passing drivers, who slowed down to watch the waddling spectacle. Dignity, I told myself, is all in the mind. It certainly wasn't anywhere else that day.

I've learned not to embarrass too easily. "What's the worst that can happen?" became my mantra, after various incidents which pretty much were the worst that could happen to an image-conscious girl, and despite my pride taking a battering I was still alive. And apparently the world was still turning. No one really cared. They were too busy trying to make sure they didn't walk into walls themselves. Freedom! Self-consciousness diminished rapidly. Though, if I'm completely honest, the occurrence of potentially embarrassing incidents didn't.

How to dig yourself into a hole when you're already underground

I once found myself on the tube, travelling through rush-hour London. Opposite me was a man who could be described by the casual observer as attractive. Had he not been fair of face the following event may not have occurred (superficiality could be to blame for so many things in my life. It's just a relief I'm so grown up these days). Anyway, when the train pulled in at a station a few stops before mine, he got up to leave. Noticing his departure, I also noticed the mobile phone left on the seat he had just vacated.

No one else was aware, possibly because their minds were set on higher things, possibly because they were asleep, unconscious or dead (it doesn't do to seem too interested on public transport). I, like a good citizen, called after the disappearing figure, "You've left your phone." He did not respond. I called again. No answer. He was getting further away. There was only one course of action.

I leapt up, grabbed the phone and ran down the carriage. By the time I caught up he was already on the platform.

"Excuse me," I called after him. He finally turned around. "You left your phone." He paused for a second, looking surprised but grateful, "Oh, thanks. That's great." Then he looked thoughtful. A longer pause. Then he pulled a phone from his pocket.

"Oh. It's not mine," he said, "but I'll hand it in to lost property on my way out."

I handed it over without hesitation (after all, he had a handsome, er, I mean, honest face) and he disappeared into the crowd. The crowd that was now getting impatient, waiting to get off or on. During the reconciliation scene no one had moved. Commuters waiting in a milling throng to board the train, and queues lining up behind me waiting to get off, all forced to watch my attempted heroics.

I turned to go back to my seat and ended up with my head in the chest of a large, angry man. I mumbled an apology for blocking his way and tried to squeeze past him. He didn't budge. I tried to wriggle round the other way. No go. I finally looked up to make eye contact. He looked down. "That", he said with what appeared to be pent-up rage rapidly about to lose its pent-ness, "was my phone."

Oh. Err... Think. Quickly.

"It wasn't on your seat," I said, with Poirot-like certainty and body language, eyebrow raised knowingly. He explained (very loudly and angrily, if you ask me) that it had fallen out of his pocket, onto the seat next to him, and when he had tried to get it back I had picked it up, run down the carriage and handed it to someone who had disappeared into the ether. Oh. No. Maybe Poirot had moments like this. Sadly we shall never know. He was no help to me now. The commuters who had been anxious to move along were suddenly in no hurry. The legendary ambivalence to the rest of humanity that personifies the world-weary Londoner was gone that day. They were rapt, all eyes on me for the next move. I paused only another second before springing into life.

"Well, don't look at me, that guy's got your phone. Get after him!" And the poor man, who had merely been minding his own business on a dull ride to work, suddenly found himself forced out into a station he had never wanted to stop at, to chase a man he had never met, to retrieve a phone he didn't know he'd lost. Probably not the start to the day he'd expected.

And that left me, planning to return quietly to my seat, to see out the rest of my journey in peace. It's a small mercy that he wasn't there to see that the only seat now free was the one he had been forced to vacate. As I turned to walk towards it, I realised that the eye contact that usually couldn't be made with fellow travellers on pain of death was now all mine – along with giggling, sniggering, loud whispering and blatant disbelief. And still three more stops to go.

"Don't worry," I announced to my new audience, with as much dignity as I could muster, "I'm not going to be helping anyone else today." And with that reassurance echoing round the carriage, I made my way to the empty seat, opposite a woman who felt the need to wink and smile reassuringly, between frequent bursts of laughter, until I could finally get off the train and pretend none of it had happened.

Mind whose own business?

Even as a teenager I had been interventionist beyond all reasonable cause. I was like the UN of the nice suburban neighbourhood I inhabited. One summer's day, spotting a kid from up the road being berated by a motorist who had stopped his car in the street and was turning purple with rage, I couldn't hold back. Stomping in, with utterly unjustified certainty, I took the side of the poor red-faced boy, who was cowering under the attack. The driver was about to deck him. Couldn't we just be reasonable? I asked. Surely whatever he'd done wasn't that bad?

I think I may have a gift in speaking too soon. It turned out that the dear boy had decided to wash the man's car. Without being asked. And without using anything other than the equipment God gave him. Yep, like a stray dog, he had marked his territory good and proper. Gallons of lemonade would have been required to complete the job – it wasn't a small car. And, being a sunny day, the windows had been open. Ah, right. I see, sir. Well, don't let me stand in your way. I must be going... You'd think by now I'd have learned some restraint. Know better than to leap in where angels, if not fearing to tread, were instead strapping on the riot gear yet again as my vigilante streak ignited over a perceived injustice? It is not for nothing my personal motto is "Never start a fight with a man with CUT HERE tattooed round his neck". I have learned the hard way.

On that day, the angels, probably rolling their eyes yet again, dispatched a couple of local likely lads to rescue me from a certain beating in the corner shop as I simply couldn't back down from informing the leather-clad, heavily tattooed, very angry man in question that there was a queue and jumping it simply wasn't the done thing. There was a stand-off while he considered which weapon to use. Into the silence burst the boys, cut short from buying the fags and beers they had ventured out to purchase, and instead hustling me out of the place with an incredulous, "Are you out of your mind?" I could only stutter in defiant response, "But he was pushing in!"

Undiplomatic incident

Possibly I've mellowed somewhat, or maybe I just don't come across so many urgent situations these days. Maybe angelic sat nav keeps me unwittingly away from routes that require self-appointed freedom fighters. Being a one-woman crime prevention roadshow aside, I have learned to think a little longer before I speak. Somewhere along the way I also learned to realise the value in sometimes saying very little and waiting for events to unfold (took some restraint, I can tell you); for people to say what they really want to say and not just what they think they should; for tiny incidents to be allowed to fade and not blow up out of all proportion. Learned the value of waiting, watching and shutting up.

Sometimes this can be the case when talking about God. If it's new to us, it's probably going to be new to a lot of the people in our lives – unless we've been surrounded by pesky Bible bashers for years and, as I've heard it so delicately put, we're the last rabbit to tumble into the pot. Are we going to start bombarding everyone around us, convinced we have to persuade everyone we meet that we have all the answers? From my own experience it didn't take much at all for people to feel uncomfortable. It was so far off most people's radar that any mention felt like a verbal assault that needed strategic defence (or usually complete avoidance). Any change of routine or priority was alarming. My pride took a few hits as I suddenly risked becoming the outsider.

I didn't want to lose the friends I'd had for years. What was to be gained from alienating those who supported and loved me? It didn't mean there weren't debates or some changes, but I did my best to keep the common ground in place. I answered questions, explained what was going on, made efforts to keep up. I guess my relocation soon after getting to know God again meant that there were more changes afoot than just what I now believed. In a new city with a new job and now trying to find a new church I was, to some degree, starting over. And that meant one big thing – explaining my new self at church and work.

Walk the line

Turn up in a church for the first time, and people may assume you're a Christian (get the time wrong, turn up halfway through a very formal service in a very traditional church and be forced by a glowering warden to sit in silence at the back for an hour before the actual meeting you came for, and people will probably assume you need help. Note to self: check times carefully). Turn up in a new company for the first time, and it won't cross anyone's mind that you're interested in anything other than their sales figures, money, living well and possibly watching X Factor of an evening.

So then what? Starting over when no one knows who you are means a perfect opportunity to present yourself however you want. But with more than one environment to negotiate, will one approach fit all? What do you do?

While your new church chums probably won't want more than a sketchy overview of what you do all day, it's equally likely your work chums won't want to know much about what happens in church, if you get round to mentioning it at all. I mean, where's the outlet? Assume you never spend time with colleagues except on work-related matters where all talk is business related, or the occasional social outing, and there may literally never be an opportunity to say anything. If, however, you do mention it to a couple of people, expect word to spread as a bit of gossip, marking you out as something of a curiosity. I would find that someone would very occasionally bring up in passing in the sandwich queue that they'd heard I was "a bit religious" or "a Bible basher" which would maybe spark a longer conversation or maybe have them snigger and scuttle off. I should probably mention at this point that at church the opposite would take place: because I didn't look like the expected template of a Christian, the scuttling and sniggering usually related to the assumption that I'd wandered in by mistake on my way to a gig. Can't win 'em all.

Who doesn't love a naked rodeo clown?

Generally business is all about, well, business, and in my working life that awful cliché work hard, play hard. On one occasion, heading out for post-work celebratory drinks (I don't remember what was being celebrated. Probably just the fact it was Friday yet again. No real reason was ever needed) a large and unruly posse of hard-working colleagues hit a local hostelry. A favourite haunt of the stressed workforce, the décor had a vaguely Wild West theme, perhaps a tribute to the general lawlessness of the clientele. The pinnacle of the interior was a life-size statue of a noble American Indian brave astride a majestic stallion, mounted on a lofty plinth in the centre of the room. He spent most of his time impassively staring past proceedings, ignored by the revellers who congregated around him knocking back cheap vodka. Little did he know tonight was his night.

Perhaps it was bonus time, perhaps he was just feeling crazy, whatever the reason, a serious-minded senior executive joined the group that evening. As he was the boss of most of those present, including me, his presence altered the dynamic somewhat. The usual anarchy was reined in as he circulated, making businessy small talk. When he and I found ourselves face to face, it came to pass that I was also facing the statue, though at that point barely noticed the man making his way onto the plinth in a very excited hurry. I doubt we'll ever know what was going through his mind when he decided his night wouldn't be complete unless he stripped butt naked, climbed onto the horse, sat astride his new bronze best friend and began a buck-a-roo routine. For the longest five minutes of my life, while trying to discuss business strategy for the coming quarter, all I could see over the shoulder of my intently listening boss was the groin of the frantically gyrating cowboy who was leaving nothing to the imagination, although thankfully his speed did create something of a blur. I still can't watch The Last of the Mohicans without occasional flashbacks.

Friends are like flowers. Sometimes you end up with a lovely bunch

Most nights out with colleagues had some similar incident. Amid the drinking and cavorting there didn't seem to be much opportunity to talk about anything meaningful. People were grabbing as much fun as they could with little interest in what might come later. And during the day, targets, pressure, meetings, presentations, travel and office politics took precedence. Lunch was a quick sandwich if it happened at all. Everyone was focused on working or living it up.

Before the grown-up days when everyone coupled off and disappeared into the suburban sunset to read the Sunday papers and reproduce, they spent much of their leisure time hammered or recovering from the effects of the hammering. The weekend would kick off with as much alcohol as they could physically manage before the pubs closed and they fell into taxis and headed home, or wherever, to sleep it off. Which meant that Saturday was a write-off. During the day, groaning and headaches. During the evening, flaking out and early night – or living it up all over again.

So for the nice Christian girl who could keep up in conversation until people started inadvertently spitting, repeating themselves and falling over, what to do? It had been years since I had hurt my liver through overconsumption and I had no desire to go back to that life. I understood how much they enjoyed it all though – I had been like that once upon a time. These days I wasn't even that bothered about a social drink or two, and I didn't really care about fitting in. But there wasn't much else going on. It was sometimes a lonely time. I spent a lot of time twiddling my proverbial thumbs, wondering if there was more to it than existing between two worlds and fitting into neither.

But somehow, somewhere in amongst all of that, friendships were formed, which are still strong to this day. Maybe it was all those trips to far-flung places for weeks on end which forced us together. Maybe it was those Saturday shopping trips when they were hung-over and I wasn't. However it happened, we got to know and like each other and in those settings conversations were had about life, love and what it might all mean. Several friends, some from the old days who had seen me change somewhat, and some who had never known any different, wanted to know more. Not immediately, but over time, when questions arose or decisions needed to be made or things didn't go to plan. They came to church. Went to Alpha. And that was it. They couldn't fit it all together. None of them felt compelled to stick around. Somehow the life they had known was what they wanted to go back to. Somehow that seemed more certain, and probably more fun.

Not many of those moments have arisen since. We're all in different situations where there just aren't opportunities to casually suggest coming along to a meeting or joining a course. Juggling babies (not literally. That takes practice), work, life in general doesn't leave time to think about much else. I sent copies of The Father's Love Letter to a few friends several years ago, with cards thanking them for being good friends, after a particularly difficult time, and each one told me they had read it and cried. Opportunities may not look the same when people are tied down with responsibilities, but in the right way we all need to know God loves us.

It's only a small can of worms

There's sometimes a moment when we could mention something deeper, suggest a helpful book or mention we'd like to pray, when we can't help but wonder if it's a good idea. I don't think I've ever said anything about God without first weighing what the outcome might be, whether now is a good time. What I don't want to do is let that slip into something else. Pride. Or maybe it's fear.

Whatever you might call it, something can hold us back when we should be getting involved. It doesn't have to be a fire and brimstone sermon (though people do love them. That look of horror is really just suppressed joy) or anything dogmatic, but it could be something someone might need to hear, especially if we've been through similar experiences. I can almost guarantee you'll know when the moment is there. When the silence is hanging, waiting for something with meaning to fill it, and helpful words come to mind, words we'd find helpful if someone said them to us. I can't honestly say I've seized every one of those moments. Not wanting to rock the boat, get knocked back, risk seeming insensitive or shutting things down more permanently. It can just seem inadequate. When intelligent people have problems, trying to talk about faith can seem like the opposite of good sense. It can sound so easy when it's talked about among Christians – what to say, even helpful diagrams that can be speedily drawn to explain the fall of man and the mechanics of salvation (great ice-breaker). But what happens when we're caught in the middle of an awkward conversation or situation? Where do we take it?

The theory is good, according to the party line (there was no party. I'm just talking about church). Explain in three easy steps who Jesus is, and it might be just what people want to hear. Well, possibly. But in most cases, when you look more closely at the people you're in relationship with, you'll find they are probably people quite like you. Similar interests, sense of humour, probably life stage. Which means you'll probably have had some similar experiences, problems and worries. And if you're a Christian, you'll have a different perspective.

Somehow we have to get to a point where that's what is at the forefront. Not trying to say the "right" thing, just sharing what we know. Our life experiences aren't wasted. When we've moved on to a new way of thinking, what's gone before isn't irrelevant. Everything we've been through is useful to someone, somewhere. It can be hard to explain how our lives have changed, when to those around us it seems a world apart. Even to those who have started out on the road, it can feel there's a long way to go.

Better the devil you know?

Martina, who hadn't been a Christian long, was struggling to understand how this transformation she kept hearing about was going to take place. While everyone at church assumed she was having a great time, she was still tempted by the same things and found it an uphill slog to stay on what seemed like the straight and narrow. There was never a good time to tell them that though. She had a Bible but didn't really read it. "I can't get into it," she said, with a shrug. "It's just, like, a really old book, about old stuff and I don't see how it has anything to do with life now."

What was helpful to her? To tell her to plough on regardless of boredom? Stick to the programme? That it isn't meant to be easy? (Or fun?) To nod sympathetically but offer no actual help? Or is there a way to help? Explain what we've learned. Find people who seem to have talent in making what's in those pages actually make sense. Talk about particular stories that seem to have some bearing on what they're going through. Look out for books which make it easy and possibly even interesting to understand. Or films which are modern allegories about God. Some people love Narnia and Lord of the Rings (I've never seen the point of a goblin, no matter how profound he may be, but each to their own). Or paintings which express something of what God is all about. If churning through the words at that early stage is preventing us getting close to God, we need to think creatively. He isn't far away. He's right there. Yes, he says he hid things for us to find (sneaky little trick, oh divine one) but we sometimes don't know how to look. We need help. It definitely doesn't hurt to ask God to show us what he's all about. I suspect he's only too keen to start giving us clues. He wants us to know him.

God-tinted spectacles

But if it seems like a slog rather than a breeze, there may be a reason for that. At the same time as wanting us close, God doesn't want us to treat him casually. When we get to know him, he wants us to really know him, and if we really know him, we're going to be different. Our issues aren't going to seem so important any more, even though we will start to realise how much we are loved. We aren't going to be impressed by the same things. We're going to start to see things his way. We start taking second place in our own lives.

And that's a scary thought.

Especially if we've grown up in a culture that tells us what we want is justified. We're individuals entitled to experiences and satisfaction. Work hard, or don't. We're consumers, but basically we're good people, not hurting anyone. Whatever we want we get. We deserve to be happy, no matter what. We find our pleasures wherever we want, and no one can tell us we shouldn't. Whatever gets you through the night.

The irony in a culture that embraces and elevates the individual is that more and more we feel part of the crowd. No matter how many social networking sites we join and update (the best way I've found to have my misadventures giggled at from Yorkshire to Yemen in a matter of minutes), no matter how much we cry out to be heard above the buzz of communication, we can easily just become part of the noise.

So why, when God wants to know us as an individual, is it so hard to let him in?

What is this relationship that people keep talking about meant to look like? Can't I just keep going as I was and hope for the best? I remember hearing about a Christian guy living in London who spent every Saturday night getting drunk and every Sunday recovering. Week in and week out, life passed by in a haze. God, he said with confidence, didn't mind. He didn't want to spoil his fun, to be a killjoy. But I'm not so sure.

Surely there had to be more to Christian life than old habits, routines and hangovers?

An inconvenient truth?

Remember this one big, kind of irritating thing (just one?) about being a Christian. One thing we probably won't like very much. One thing that's hard to get away from... Ready? One thing that we have to say goodbye to is our pride. (Give it up? But my pride is better than everyone else's!) You may still come across certain behaviours in church that could be described as pride (and I'm not talking about those who choose not to change), but they will generally have a very different focus to the things people who aren't Christians get excited about. These often involve people talking about what sets them apart in the Christian world. When they say they've got an amazing gift, don't ask them if they got it for their birthday. What they mean is that they think God has been really kind to them and given them an extra portion of something special. Not cake – though I would probably have difficulty keeping quiet about that too – but something that they think they can use to show off more about God. A great ability to dance. A special affinity with children. A talent for speaking in public. Things that might set them apart among non-Christians too, should they venture out of church to try them out, but things they want to use in a positive and healthy way no matter what the location.

God doesn't have the same priorities or concerns as we do about looking good in front of everyone we meet. We have to be prepared to not necessarily look our best, and I'm not talking about physical appearance. I mean not living with the same motivations we used to. We may still go out, have social lives, shop, eat well, enjoy ourselves, but it should feel different. I don't mean wrong. I guess for me it just wasn't the point any more. I still loved dancing the night away but it couldn't be the thing I lived for. I couldn't go out every night and make just enjoying myself the only priority. If

God had something else going on that day, I didn't want to miss it. This is about someone else's priorities taking over. The Bible doesn't mess about. It refers to dying to self. Doesn't sound like fun. I'm not sure they mention it when you pop in to church for those special meetings designed for people wondering about God. I think they save it for later, when you're already convinced and you've exchanged the visitor's pass for full membership. But why would God want us to do that? Because he wants our full attention. Not a place in our hearts while our priorities stay the same as they've always been, but a radical re-shaping. Eek. That sounds painful. And it is, because we're very attached to what we had before, even if we weren't enjoying it very much really. Or maybe we were, but something we heard about God couldn't be ignored. In the search for meaning, we've found ourselves here, sitting on God's doorstep wondering what now?

Deafening silence

Never mind navigating church and those strange people, what about the other stuff? The stuff they expect you to do during the week when no one's around. The "relationship" stuff. The praying. The "quiet time". The meditation. The Bible reading. The assumption that now you've met God, you've got loads to say to him. That he'll be chatting away to you too, if only you knew what he sounded like. Or maybe you've been told that a quiet time is just that – quiet. It was a concept that made me want to run a mile when I first heard about it. Not only was I not living it up like my colleagues and chums, when I got home I was supposed to not watch TV, not phone people, not lie on the sofa and stare into space. I was meant to have A Quiet Time. It just sounded so naff. Boring. The sort of thing involving time travel to an era when women in flowing skirts would live in their simply decorated homes with lots of framed Bible verses and soft, churchy music playing, while they sat cross-legged and barefoot, earnestly smiling in holy bliss. Or the more modern equivalent, which still involves the smiling, but this time by women who still wear flowery hair clips regardless of their age and who call everything awesome (no offence if you're sporting a snazzy hair accessory as you read this. It looks stunning. Honest). It just wasn't my cup of tea. If this was where the brainwashing started and the caring about everything but reading my Bible stopped, I didn't want to know.

Pride on my part? Maybe a tiny, wee bit (maybe a bit more than that. Told you I was proud of my pride). And probably horribly judgemental about girly fashions too. But the way it was explained to me made it sound like a chore that everyone else found a joy. First there was the idea that God was only chatty in the mornings. Start your day "in the word", whatever that meant. The gist seemed to be getting up very early and meditating oneself into heavenly bliss – or at least some kind of exercise in comprehension of religious texts. I am not, as almost anyone who has ever spent more than a day with me will testify, a morning person. It would take a fog horn, a bulldozer and possibly the threat of violence to move me before sunrise. Even during my corporate life, I was not an early riser, despite the impact on my professional reputation compared to those who were at their desks at the unearthly time of six, eight or nine am. I mean, who were they trying to impress?

Evensong works for me

Having learned to respect my body clock I don't force the issue any more. It's just not worth it. If I am at my most alert when everyone else is in the land of nod, so be it. Gone are the days when I drag myself up, half an hour earlier than my body is expecting, waiting for the heavens to serenade me. It had the appearance of a Jekyll and Hyde metamorphosis – propping myself against a wall, while my head slumped forward and the words blurred as I struggled to keep my eyes open. Beneficial, I suspect, to no one. Get one of those "thought for the day" type publications if you feel the need for edification in the morning but your body clock won't co-operate. Don't get on a guilt trip because you're not on the stairway to heaven as the sun rises.

There seems to be a little more understanding for the nocturnal these days. It's apparently OK to pick a later time to switch off the outside world and plug into the heavenly realms instead. So what should you do? In some respects, don't worry about it. It really is a genuinely good idea to remove all outward distractions and shut out everything that demands your time for a while each day. Even people who don't believe in God will tell you that, although they may not actually do it themselves. It may be a good idea to find some music that makes you feel connected to God somehow. If you're the type of person who can't hear a tune they like without dancing, or singing along, do that. If you just appreciate the silence, switch your phone off and get some ear plugs. Get comfortable. If you're prone to drifting off, as I am, try not to make it too comfortable – not every day anyway.

Lie back and think of spreadsheets

Back in my working life I was sometimes forced to attend very, very dull meetings. They involved spreadsheets which seemed to have no purpose and no end, and a man who explained them, who seemed capable of going on indefinitely (he was also in the office by five am each day. That should tell you all you need to know). It would be fair to say I was there under some duress. The designated half-hour slot for him to talk about the spreadsheet was to be endured in a notoriously cold meeting room. I, as well as being not at my best in the morning, am also not great when it's cold. (I know what you're thinking – if you ever need rescuing from a snowy mountain at daybreak, I'm top of your list to call. Oh, I don't like heights either. Anyway, I digress...) This particular day, I wasn't prepared to sit through another shivering half hour of boredom with no recourse. It was hard enough to take it all in when icicles were forming on the end of my nose. I managed to find a fleecy blanket kicking around the office and decided to take it into the meeting with me. I was sure I could think of a good excuse if challenged. Call it an executive toy or something. One that was worn around the shoulders.

So off I went, fully prepared and possibly quite jet-lagged. Or maybe it was plain old tiredness from having to get up in the middle of the night to read Psalms. Whatever the reason, I found myself less than alert. As the spreadsheet man began his weekly monologue, the warmth of the blanket and the drone of the voice combined to devastating effect. I fell asleep. Sitting in the chair, leaning back, dead to the world. Excusable perhaps, except for the fact I was now fully wrapped in the blanket, like a swaddled baby Jesus or a caterpillar cocoon. It didn't look like a spur of the moment happening. It looked much more like some kind of surreal protest, and totally premeditated at that. It didn't end well. No one likes to be woken up by shouting.

Book club

If you're trying to work out how to connect with God with your eyes open, the Bible is ideal (see what a great selling job I did there? I'm well on the way to getting my commission this month). There are many different translations, which means you don't need to be stuck with something that you can't relate to. Some people like the Ye and Thus of the King James, some like the Hey Guys vibe of The Message, and there are many in between. They all have the same basic content, but different tones and levels of formality. I've embraced a phone version, so it's there if I have a few spare minutes during the day. Read a few before you get one – it helps not to have something you dread picking up because the language seems so alien. (If you pick one up and it features aliens, that's probably not the one to go for – we don't learn about aliens till we reach level 4.)

Some people swear by a study guide (in the very nice Christian way of swearing, obviously), which highlights a section to read each day, usually with some kind of explanation or modern application. Some prefer to just read and interpret for themselves. If you start on your own and find it overwhelming or confusing (or boring), it's probably a good idea to have something to hand to make it easier (alcohol is generally considered a last resort). Study Bibles actually contain a lot of extra info to provide context, and can make what you're reading much easier to understand. It might help to talk about it with people who've been at it longer than you, too. I've noticed that often we are all still figuring it out, and there can be many meanings to what seems like a simple story. It's good to have input from others who may have a different insight, and to find out how different parts connect. While some parts can seem to be nothing more than lists of names in ancient Middle Eastern history, I think you'll be surprised at some of the other things you'll find. There are lots of intriguing stories and hidden meanings waiting to be discovered.

Promise.

Give yourself a break

I've found it's helpful not to waste time comparing yourself to others in how long you're spending connecting with God. As a general rule, I'd aim for around half an hour a day. Did you just gasp? The length of a whole episode of Coronation Street/ EastEnders/Hollyoaks? (Delete as applicable, though if you're left with Hollyoaks we may need to have words.) It's just a suggestion. Any less and it's easy not to really start. It takes a while to tune out of the day, to do lists, what you're going to have for dinner, who you need to call. If you start at half an hour and want to spend longer, do it. If you really need to stop after fifteen minutes it's not the end of the world. I wish I could tell you there's a switch to flick and it all falls into place. Generally it's trial and hopefully not too much error, but at least some wondering why you're doing this, feeling hungry or distracted, irritated that nothing seems to be happening, bored. I'm just trying to be honest so that if you've felt that way and everyone you meet in church tells you how great it is to spend time with God and how much they get out of it and how much it flows, you'll at least know that some of us struggle to get there. There are days when it's not like that, and I'd encourage you to carry on till you reach that point. I don't think explaining how I feel on a "good day" would help, as it's a really personal thing, but I have been helped by writers like Mark Virkler, who have devoted years to understanding how to hear God's voice and help people to do the same.

We all have different ways of communicating with each other; some of us are more visual than others. Learn from others, but don't rely on their experiences instead of having your own. The notion that God wanted to speak directly to each of us was a radical concept hundreds of years ago, when people had only ever expected to be told what to do by a priest. Today claiming to hear from God could spark the interest of mental health professionals. It doesn't seem to have been a straightforward topic since Bible times. Some of us are still struggling with it now, and maybe when we spend our days busy, working and stretched, we shouldn't be expecting our experiences to match up with those who stand at the front of church and preach (though some of those might tell you they struggle too sometimes). God knows where each one of us is at – we don't need to be too embarrassed to admit it.

As we go about our lives, God will still be speaking to us. Through the time we spend tuning everything else out, even if we don't realise it, we are still getting close to God. He wants us to know him for real, not to assume that we do. We may be in for a few surprises. When we're used to a world of image and celebrity, starting to see things God's way can be strange. His priorities are not our priorities. He doesn't do things our way. In life we're going for bigger, better, faster, fitter, shinier, smarter – and God isn't. At least not in ways we understand. We may think we have the answers but often we're not even asking the right questions. It can all look a little bit weird sometimes, not at all what we had in mind.

It was a dark and funky night

A few years ago I had something of an addiction. Nothing that would have landed me in the Priory but not part of the standard Christian lifestyle either. There was nothing I loved more than ripping up a dance floor and putting Madonna to shame (through being a better dancer, that is. My conical bra usually stayed at home). It was not unheard of for people to come up and ask, awestruck, to learn my moves (they may have been drunk but I think alcohol just heightened their awareness of genius). There were countless clubs I could have honoured with my jiving presence but one place always got my vote. Time after time, my dancing partner in crime and I would make our way up a dingy staircase, through a fluorescently lit Chinese restaurant, to a shadowy, slightly bowed dance floor which was barely occupied. A lone figure in the corner, hidden by a set of flashing lights in primary colours, would announce a classic disco anthem, and from the darkness surrounding the floor figures would suddenly appear. The empty floor filled with crazy moves as people who loved to dance launched into their finest routines. We stayed there for hours, surrounded by a crowd who willingly neglected every other venue in town to make their way to what should have been a disaster.

But somehow the combination of people who loved to dance, whatever music we asked for, a dance floor that was only used for dancing and not for people trying to cop off, and some magic ingredient that perhaps only makeshift discos hiding at the back of Chinese restaurants possess, made it an amazing experience every time we went there. But try and explain to people that you spent the evening in the back room of such a place, twirling away while waiters carrying bowls of noodles did their best not to get knocked over, and they will think you're joking. But it was true. It shouldn't have worked but it did. It was the opposite of everything a good night out should have consisted of, but it was the best time to be had in town.

Tenuous it may be but I think that's how God is sometimes. We think we know what it should all look like, have it all planned out, the perfect blueprint of what's going to work for us.

And he tears it up. Has a better idea.

It won't necessarily involve dodging bowls of special fried rice as you spin to the tunes of DJs who'd be more at home in a working men's club, but it will definitely be surprising.

Until we meet again...

And so, the time has come to say farewell – for now. We've talked with great seriousness and profound, possibly world-changing insight about life, love and the dramas in between. Wondered if there is a right way to do things, and if anyone will notice if we don't do it. Reviewed rather a lot of evidence relating to the fact that I don't always learn from my own mistakes – though I do seem to have 20/20 hindsight. Realised that I'm still figuring out the best way to do pretty much everything, and so are most people I know. Spotted that life has some interesting twists and turns, and often a few speed bumps along the way. Hopefully concluded that redemption is never far away and something called grace can't wait to save the day.

So what about you? Have you found yourself in the same situations, asked the same questions, given in to – or even resisted – the same temptations and you're still wondering what it's all about? Are you thinking that this has been an interesting (or not), slightly bizarre glimpse into the world of a girl who is a fan of Jesus, eyeliner, second chances, and the occasional act of mischief, but what does it all have to do with you? Maybe you've figured out life your own way, what it all means and how you want to live it. Maybe you're still wondering if there's more to discover, whether there's more to life than just being good. In my very personal opinion, I think there always is, and it probably doesn't look like the plans we've made for ourselves. Is it worth the risk of finding out? Are you ready for your own adventure?